DUST GLO.

DUST GLORIFIED
An Anthology and Personal Testament

by Anne Shells

Foreword
by Martin Israel

Shoreline Books
Bristol

First published by Shoreline Books 1992

Selection and compiler's contributions © 1992 Anne Shells

Extract from *A Brief History of Time* by Stephen Hawking, published by Bantam Press, © Space Time Publications 1988: all rights reserved. Permission is also gratefully acknowledged for the use of copyright material from the following: *The Bhagavad Gita* translated by Juan Mascaro (Penguin Books Ltd); *Library Looking Glass* by David Cecil (Constable Publishers); *Simple Prayer* by John Dalrymple (Darton Longman & Todd Ltd); *Hymne de l'univers* by Teilhard de Chardin (Editions du Seuil); 'Miss T' by Walter de la Mare (the Literary Trustees of Walter de la Mare and The Society of Authors as their representative); 'Peck of Gold' from *The Poetry of Robert Frost* edited by Edward Connery Lathem (Random Century Group); *Seven to Flee and Seven to Follow* by Richard Holloway (Cassell plc); *Night Thoughts* by Martin Israel (SPCK); *Revelations of Divine Love* by Julian of Norwich translated by Clifton Wolters (Penguin Books Ltd); *The Go-Between God* by John V. Taylor (SCM Press Ltd); *Face to Face* by Frances Young (T & T Clark Ltd). Every effort has been made to trace copyright owners. If any item has been overlooked, the publishers would be glad to be notified so that this can be rectified in any future edition.

Photographs: 'Dust' by Mike Fear, Photographer, Watlington, Oxfordshire; 'Stars' by Nigel Metcalfe, Department of Physics, University of Durham (by courtesy of the Royal Greenwich Observatory who own the equipment used).

Cover picture: detail of the Altarpiece, 'The Annunciation, with St Emidius' by Carlo Crivelli, reproduced by courtesy of the Trustees of the National Gallery, London

Printed and bound in Great Britain by BPCC Wheatons Ltd, Exeter
Cover printed by Doveton Press Ltd, Bristol

British Library Cataloguing-in-Publication Data
A catalogue record for this book is available from the British Library.

ISBN 1 873229 07 0

Shoreline Books
11 Colston Yard, Colston Street, Bristol BS1 5BD, England

Contents

Foreword	7
Preface	9
Introduction	11
But First the Crumbs	17
Part I: Plot of Dust and Soul	27
Part II: This Speck of Dust Glorified	67
Part III: Exult, O Dust and Ashes	75
Appendix	96

Illustrations

Dust	48
Stars – see the Appendix	49

To the children of Barnham Street Buildings
and Vine Street Buildings
– either side of Tooley Street in Bermondsey –
during the years 1941 to 1953.
And to my grandchildren today.

Foreword

Anne Shells' experience in life is the basis of this fine anthology, *Dust Glorified*, which has as its theme dust and its renewal through love. Nothing that has been made is without some meaning in the greater scheme of life, even if at first sight it appears merely destructive, such as the organisms which cause diseases in plants and animals, including the human being. By love their higher message may be understood, so that the havoc wrought by so many of life's vicissitudes may in the end be the way from mere selfish preoccupation to communal sharing. This finds its fuller expression in the love that is of God the Creator.

Everything is made by God, whose sun shines on good and bad alike, and whose rain falls equally on the just and the unjust. We hope for the time when all creation will flow into mutual service, when moral distinctions cease inasmuch as all actions are dedicated to the common good in the service of God.

It is reflections like these that come to my mind as I read Anne's anthology of hope, which I believe will be of support to many who are experiencing their own travail as a preparation for their release into light, the light of God's creative love.

Martin Israel

Preface

It is wonderful to have a chance to thank people publicly for all the help I have been given to achieve this book. Alas, if I took it, there would have to be yet another chapter. But I must mention Marion Morgan for taking the risk of publishing it, Liz Rees for getting it into order, and Penny Saunders among so many for constant encouragement.

And my husband, Charles, of course.

A.S.

Introduction

Ah, make the most of what we yet may spend,
  Before we too into the Dust descend,
  Dust into Dust, and under Dust to be
Sans wine, sans Song, sans Singer, and sans End!

Rubaiyat of Omar Khayyam

And we are put on earth a little space,
That we may learn to bear the beams of love;

William Blake, 'The Little Black Boy'

Remember, man, that dust thou art –
Dust, by the spirit stung to life;
Yea, recollect thyself a part
          of the eternal strife.

Remember, then, with healing pain
Thy graceless other worldly mood;
Turn to the living earth again,
And thou shalt find her good.

Evelyn Underhill,
First and Last Verses of Memento Homo

'Tis the sublime of man
Our noontide majesty, to know ourselves
Parts and proportions of the wondrous whole.

Samuel Taylor Coleridge

The Bible looks forward to God re-creating the world, resurrecting humanity to a new life, in some sense continuous with this, and yet transformed. That I think is where we can find a true Christian hope for the future. I do not think we have immortal souls. I think we are frail creatures of dust and every one of us needs renewal and healing, re-making in fact. We are in the same case as the handicapped. Our present existence is the 'seed' of a new existence. 'Someone will ask, How are the dead raised? With what kind of body do they come? . . . What you sow is not the body which is to be, but a bare kernel. So it is with the resurrection of the dead. What is sown is perishable, what is raised is imperishable. It is sown in weakness, it is raised in power . . . Lo, I tell you a mystery. We shall not all sleep, but we shall all be changed . . .'
1 Cor.15: 35-52.

Frances Young, *Face to Face*

It is a great mystical saying that there is nothing in this world that is unholy, there is only that which has not yet been blessed. This is incidentally not merely a Christian insight but a Jewish insight. It is one of the reported aspects of the Jewish way which Jesus himself inherited and transformed. That is why Peter was shown in his dream that there is nothing clean or unclean at all. Everything has been made by God. And we in our own way through the power of blessing are to change that which is corruptible to that which is incorruptible. That is the great spiritual lesson. That we go about in the world in whatever form God has consecrated us . . . in joy and thanksgiving.

Martin Israel, *Summons to Life*

... that God, by means of an inner divine illumination, acts upon the soul like the rays of the sun. When these shine through a window they illuminate countless atoms floating in the air and hitherto invisible. Happy the soul that God deigns thus to enlighten on the infinite mysteries of the interior life!

de Caussade, *Progress in Prayer*

This made it the more likely that he had seen a true vision; for instead of making common things look commonplace as a false vision would have done, it had made common things disclose the wonderful that was in them.

George Macdonald, *The Shadows*

What the inspiration of the Holy Spirit brings is a new understanding of God's glory as made evident in the incarnation of His son, Jesus Christ.

Martin Israel, *Night Thoughts*

The purpose of this testament-cum-anthology is to bring the illumination of love to those who read it, and by this light find the transforming power of love in daily life. It would be too glorious an aim were it not initiated by trust in God and belief in the value of 'living' books. That is why it is a mixture of quotations from many writers with my own contributions. I could not do it alone.

By 'living' books I mean those that help me to live my own particular life with its ups and downs. The writers are more than mere authors, they are 'living' friends. They speak aloud to me, stir me up, give me a poke and shove, inspire me, and in the end proclaim that 'it is from the hushed heart flows love': 'she that trusts in Me, from her deepest heart shall rivers of life flow forth'.

Illumination of why we are, and faith that in the end all creation is destined for transformation into glory – these are what give meaning to the word Resurrection. That life is so full of tragedy, horror, crime and sin, dirt and despair, darkness, fear, anxiety, dread, enables us to realise the magnitude of that transformation. That we can glimpse such things is due to the incarnation of Jesus Christ. Jesus said: 'Peace is my parting gift to you, my own peace, such as the world cannot give. Set your troubled hearts at rest . . .' (John 14.27).

Christ's gift of peace often seems to be beyond our horizons, buried too deep to be found. But His life, that ended in such failure, shows us the truth. It also shows us the way and that we have in every moment the help of the Holy Spirit, who pours forth grace into every corner of human hearts.

We have to accept this grace into ourselves; we are exactly like a leaf on any tree, or any blade of grass, in need of turning to the light. The leaf and the blade of grass do it by the laws of the universe; we do it by an act of will from our position of freedom to choose. God has put It-Him-Herself into our hands. He actually does need our co-operation!

We have work to do and no time to lose. Please read on! I have much love and hope to share with you. As a bowl of pebbles makes us want to get down to the beach to make our own discoveries, so I believe anthologies have a place on our bookshelves.

As to being an author of a book: it is to share authenticity. So I believe everyone has a book within them, the sharing of their own unique and marvellous experience of one life. Fortunately it is not only authors who can do this, in their books, but everyone in their daily living, in their own particular life span, however long or however short.

> Till I go to dust
> In God I'll trust.

But First the Crumbs

Just when this book was all finished and I was enjoying the relief – a phone call: 'Would you write in a bit more, not your thoughts or quotations but your life?'

Being polite and wanting to please – that has been a lifetime trouble – I said: 'Oh, yes, of course – what sort of thing?'

'Well, about how you got into going from Devon to Bermondsey.'

'You mean Scrubs prison, Blenheim Palace? The War?'

My publisher is such a nice person, but she doesn't know me all that well and I had not mentioned those experiences before. People are always, not surprisingly, taken aback and confused when I say I've been in Wormwood Scrubs for a year. And in any case, one doesn't normally go back to the past. It's all a very, very long time ago.

She was a bit taken aback, as I expected.

'Well, a chapter more of some sort or other,' she said. 'After all, the book is going to cost quite a lot and you owe it to those who buy it to give a bit more autobiography!'

Stupidly, I said: 'Of course, no problem.'

But it is. I'm flummoxed.

Go back to the beautiful house and garden of my Devonshire childhood? (Old Mrs Ash telling me about Jesus.) The influence of an extraordinary boarding-school in Bournemouth? (Headmistress rubbing my back violently: 'Jellyfish! I can't feel any backbone!') Wonderful summer holidays, boating, bathing, picnics, dancing, tennis, and lovely empty years that followed?

What does she want? What can she mean? The agonising over a career?

'I think you ought to live at home and not take a job; there is so much unemployment you would be doing a girl out of work who needed it.' That's what my father genuinely thought. I tried to please him, of course, and dithered. University was never mentioned. My mother said she had some unexpected money that would pay for me to go to a 'finishing school' in Paris. So I learnt how to say 'les yeux bleus' with a perfect French accent and have hats specially made for me, trail round every museum in Paris and attend the Opéra for a five-hour performance of *Tristan and Isolde*, which Madame said we should not go to unless we knew what it was to be in love. There was no hope of that, for which we eight girls longed: we never spoke to man or boy, except the piano teacher who drove me to play the whole of the *Moonlight Sonata* (not just the first movement), making sure I realised that I was not up to it.

Back in Devon, the sophisticated ways that I had acquired were completely useless, and after some more dithering weeks I went to London to learn dress-making in Bond Street. New opportunities for going out and around and boy friends became a priority and a mystery. I had but little understanding of how to cope. Conventions were very different then from now. But it always strikes me as odd that there is nothing about love affairs in the Litany! Or much mention in church of such problems until you are confronted with an irrevocable 'for richer for poorer, for better for worse'.

This full London experience ended, and I was back home again, attempting to set up on my own. It was definitely not a success, but culminated with an aged aristocrat, who annually attended at Court for the Presentations, wanting a 'new train of silver lace over royal blue georgette, dear, and no one will know it is the dress I wore last year – and the year before!' It gave me a somewhat cheating opportunity to call myself a 'Court Dressmaker'! And I clearly remember the day I drove 30 miles across Devon to deliver it at the last moment. On arrival: 'There's a phone message for you, your father needs the car, you are to pick him up and take him home.' Another dash through hair-raising lanes to a remote rectory where there was a meeting to discuss the new Oxford Group Movement. Adept at social lies, I could think up nothing better than to say: 'I'm sorry, I forgot.' I was escorted into this roomful of clergy by the enthusiastic elderly daughter, who ran the parish for her ancient father. She said: 'Look, Anne has the real Oxford Group spirit, she has told the truth – she forgot'. They clapped. My poor father gave me a wink.

'How did you get there?' I asked him when back in the car.

'Well,' he said, 'the fact is I forgot all about it too, but when they rang up I said I was waiting for you to come back. They insisted on fetching me over.'

Inevitably I got let in for running the Sunday School with an old man who was a British Israelite and Enid. I guess Enid kept the whole thing going. We met in a medieval village hall and there was one family who had run out of names and called the last two boys Morris and Austin: although no one had cars, all were proud of the car industry. One afternoon my boy-friend flew over in a little plane and looped the loop. We all dashed out and waved. He became a pilot in the Battle of Britain.

We found it hard to believe the war would really come. My friends joined the Wrens, but I thought I would look awful in uniform, being short and dumpy, and signed on to do canteen work with the Metropolitan Police, with no idea what it entailed. And found myself in Scrubs prison a day before war was declared. There was an amnesty for the prisoners and they all streamed out. A stream of furniture vans drove in. Lino was put down, telephones were installed, desks and chairs brought in and cells transformed into 'offices'. A huge tent, for use as a canteen, was erected between Block B and Block C, and hordes of civil servants, Service personnel (a few VIPs and other ranks), new call-ups training to censor mail, and others all came in for meals.

Later we used the concert room, the bake house and another large place near the kitchen. The smell was appalling.

At the back of the tent was an ancient burner to boil up the water. George was in charge. He had been a clown and had nowhere to go and would not be fit to fight. He and Jock, another aged ex-prisoner, did everything together. I was waiting beside George while he made the tea by tipping a packet into a bucket, pouring the boiling water over it, and stirring it round with a broom handle. (It was our job to balance on a stool and tip it into a shiny urn hoping no one was looking. And then see how quickly one could pour out a tray-load of thick white cups.) When they cleared the cells, it created three mountainous heaps of tin jugs, bowls and jerries. As I stood waiting with George, Jock came up beaming: 'Look 'ere what I got.' He produced a jerry from under his coat. George eyed it solemnly. 'Sure it's a good fit?' Anything that made for any sort of laugh was welcome that first day of the war.

We worked so hard, and such long hours, it was incredible. The crocks were very heavy. Someone worked out we carried over half a ton during the lunch period only. And we walked miles. I reckoned scrubbing out a Scrubs 'bog' was about the filthiest job I had had to do up to that date. And the cockroaches! But we laughed all day and had fun. The 'top brass' personnel were always teasing and kind, but we amazed the snooty secretaries by answering them back and treating them with some disdain if they were rude to us. It has been a lifelong joy to know what it is like to be a char and a waitress.

These various War Office departments were all a cover for MI5 as everyone now knows. But then we signed the Official Secrets Act. I was out doing a round of the cells with bananas and choc-bars (plentiful for a few weeks) and somehow never did. I nursed this secret for years; it was an offence not to sign, but I quite liked trusting myself. Everyone went home in the evening except six of us girls, who slept in the evacuated warders' (prison officers') quarters. It was appallingly uncomfortable and drab. We were supposed to sleep in the cells of A Block if there was an air raid, but once was enough and we took a chance and stayed in bed. After several incendiary attacks (we rushed round dropping dustbin lids on them where we could), we were told to pack our bags and be off at 6.30a.m. Four of us, the advance party, were driven in a jeep to an unknown destination.

It turned out to be Blenheim Palace!

We were billetted in the Home Park Farm. It was completely cold and empty at 10 o'clock that lovely September morning. So we went wooding and lit all the fires, borrowed a broom from a cottage nearby and swept through. We were a bit hysterical with it all when a tall and very elegant lady arrived with two tall daughters and dogs.

'Miss Lethbridge?' she said, 'I am the Duchess of Marlborough. Is there anything we can do for you?' 'Oh, yes,' I said, 'we are starving.' 'Come and have lunch with the Duke and me,' she said. And so the other three went off in their overalls and were waited on by a parlour maid wearing white gloves. They had corn on the cob for the first time (it was a new fashion), with gold prongs to hold them, and enjoyed themselves. I waited for a few tatty mattresses and some crockery and a kettle. Later the Duchess used to ask us in for a drink and help her play with Blandford who was about seven.

It was just as hard work as at the Scrubs, and there was no time to explore the beautiful parkland. Sometimes we got a hitch to Oxford for a spree.

On one such occasion, I went to a solemn and hilarious meeting about the Blitz and conditions in South London where the air raids were bad. The talk was given by a chain-smoking, astounding woman sitting on the floor with her Pekinese dog, Funny, on her lap. She was a brilliant and witty speaker, Daisy Knight Bruce (usually known as KB). She was looking for volunteers to be air raid wardens for 61 Arch along Tooley Street near London Bridge. No one spoke up. So because of my trying-to-please upbringing ('Be responsible!') I offered myself, thinking it couldn't be worse than canteen work and all the washing-up (detergents had not been invented), although being a barmaid was fun.

That was how I got from Devon to Bermondsey.

KB had Devonshire roots herself. I owe her more than anyone in my whole life for her talk that evening, for her own unique brand of Christianity. I wrote a description of her memorial service that was published in *This Most Amazing Day* compiled by Christopher Herbert.

Bermondsey 1941

That first day? Standing cluelessly in Oxford Street, wondering what bus to catch? I hailed a taxi scared stiff I would be jeered at on arrival. In fact the street was deserted when I arrived at the Time and Talents Settlement where I was to be put up for a time. Mary Turner came to the door, gave me a cuppa (new word) and asked if I could help her sort out some jumble. Somewhat shaken I said, 'Of course, quite an expert actually, but I thought I was going to do something exciting to do with shelters.'

'Oh, I am to take you down tonight,' Mary said. 'Look, you had better take this sleeping-bag with you. I won't be able to stay.'

'What am I supposed to do?'

'I haven't the foggiest!' she said. 'There are hundreds of people sleeping there.'

So about 9.00 p.m. we walked down Bermondsey Street and stepped through a little door into an immense place: 61 Arch, lofty as a cathedral but windowless. Stainer's Arch, next door, had had a direct hit the week before with tremendous loss of life and casualties. Mary introduced me to two night duty nurses and went off.

They gave me a cuppa and chatted.

'What am I supposed to do?' I asked.

'We've no idea,' said one. 'I should tuck up and go to sleep in the wash-room. It never gets used – the taps don't work. You'll need another blanket, it gets dreadfully cold in here.' I thought I was living a Dickensian nightmare. The trains rumbled overhead.

But the sirens never went off all night.

Of course the whole time turned into a marvellous experience. I could write on and on and have you in stitches – and tears.

Thank you KB for coming to Oxford that cold evening in a blacked-out freezing train.

People will tell you the war years were 'good times' (if you survived); but my brand of 'war work' was one of endlessly *learning*, of new and amazing experiences with people. I ended up, among other things, responsible for a children's club (many evacuees returned) and realised there was a need for such places because hundreds and hundreds of children had absolutely nowhere to play on their own. (And there still is this great need in the 1990s.) But meanwhile I had another treat in store. I was allowed to leave 'war work' and go to the London School of Economics, and at the advanced age of 27 began to be educated in economics, social history, basic psychology, philosophy and – because of knowing the Scrubs blindfold – criminology and penology. (Our lot were guinea pigs for this famous course with Hermann Mannheim.) It has meant constant interest in our prisons, and continual shock that so little is done about reform.

LSE was evacuated to Cambridge and then returned to London. I was lucky to have a year of each. The war ended; so did a possible marriage hope. I was now a professional social worker about to do work where it was vital that this should not be known! After an interlude back in Devon, I returned to Bermondsey in 1947 to run the Children's Flats experiment. And that is another story. It was a much harder decision to go back the second time, but became an enriching experience beyond imagination.

In 1954 I married Charles Shells. And that, too, is another story.

My dear publisher, you asked for a slice more of my life. It is less than a slice – a few crumbs picked out from a huge, rich cake of memories. It has given me a sense of survival, especially from childhood confusions that still have a power to haunt and influence. Being born on a Friday was such a terrible burden! I must be 'loving and giving'. I was not 'fair of face', nor had 'far to go', was spared working 'hard for a living' and thankfully not 'a child of woe'. Pity the Wednesday child, but Friday's child needs some pity too: it is a fearful ideal.

And born in 1917.

When I was about ten years old, the family doctor told me it was a vintage year for babies. I felt as though I was reprieved for all the failure and guilt I felt about myself as a child, but didn't like to ask him what a vintage was. But I knew it meant a lot to me to have been born that terrible year of suffering. Somehow I had to compensate for all the slaughter, the appalling horrors.

I do not believe we have yet 'come through' the First World War; it is taking a hundred years.

Much later in life I discovered that Charles Peguy was killed in France the week that I was born. Charles Peguy! Who understood poverty, was inspired by Joan of Arc and loved the Beauce, that amazing flat area all around Chartres Cathedral.

I have found a sort of determination in being part of this date in history.

And there is no space here to share my love for Margaret of Scotland, queen and saint, who walked out of a picture-book and took me by the hand when, aged seven, I was having my tonsils out in a lonely nursing-home. Much later in life, Julian of Norwich came to my rescue and has stayed beside me ever since.

You do see what I mean? That everything ties up? All our days, empty or full, belong in the vast expanse of love that must be the heart of Christ in time and out of time.

The weight, the vision, of glory must always outweigh the suffering and hells of evil that have happened in my life's spell.

And still happen.

We may lose sight of glory over and over again, but that does not mean that the glory is not there.

The American Indians treat every blade of grass with reverence.

Joseph of Cupertino saw God in one daisy.

I saw the Incarnation in one speck of dust.

This encompasses all the times when one may feel worthless, unwanted. The days when we feel everything is all nothingness. How can 'I' be anyone? Among the teeming millions of mankind, the countless stars, what does it all amount to? Our humanity requires us to experience frustration and despair, loss and depression.

I would like to sum it up for you in 'The Squashed Grape'.

> You trod on me, God.
> I know You didn't mean to
> I got in the way –
> just the other day –
> You trod on me, God.
>
> It wasn't your fault
> (or mine for that matter)
> what a splatter
> squash – flat.
> You trod on me, God,
> and that's that.

But how now?
I know you care, aware,
and I need to get up.
It's no fun being flat,
and I am right down,
squashed flat.
A lot of people are
treading on me now
so how about that?

***

Listen to me, get it right.
Who do you think you are? God said.
Listen! I need you as wine
You were a grape off my vine,
I pressed you flat in my vat.

***

Oh, that's fine, I said,
that's fine.
And God said: *You can forget the pain*
and be Champagne.
Champagne? I said to God
Am I that good?
Yes, said God, *That's understood,*
You're the best wine
When you are mine.

PART I

Plot of Dust and Soul

This book is conceived as a sort of plait. There are three distinct threads woven together.

One strand is the description of how dust became glorified for me. It happened once in a moment out of time. One speck of dust became a precious event. It was also an illumination and a revelation. It is only now, over half a century later, that I feel the time is right to share the experience; that I *should* share it. It has instant recall and is not subject to the vagaries of memory. It was a simple moment; there was nothing about it that was anything but gentle, quiet, loving. It was a complete moment. There was everything before and now all these years later, there is everything since. But in this moment now, as I write to you, I find it just as it was: simply, gently, lovingly complete.

I want to share it simply, gently, lovingly, trustingly, just as it was, with this glorious inspiration of the incarnation of God in all his works.

The second strand is culled from a brief anthology that I have collected about dust. I have developed a sympathy with those poets and scientists and others who have found a creative discovery about dust to work upon. Dust and death, of course!

The third strand is belief in God's voice speaking through his saints, especially Julian of Norwich – in the words of George Herbert, that 'silk twist let down from heav'n'. But also many others from the past and today. These saintly voices speak of how heaven comes to earth and how earth leads to heaven.

But because life is never neat or tidy or without its constant proneness to sin and failure, the plait frequently gets unwound and blown all over the place. This can't be helped. My hair was plaited in pigtails throughout my school days, so I should know what happens to plaits and how difficult it is to achieve successful ones.

The analogy of rope would have been just as good. The point is that courage and hope in living this life come through the intertwining of experience and encouragement, learning to trust each other and God. We are all in this together. An awareness of the Company of Heaven, the Cloud of Witnesses, is cause for celebration and thanksgiving. They probably keep an eye on our journey towards them. Such speculation cannot be out of place. There are many intimations of its relevance.

About the anthology strand: at first I thought there was a distinction to be made among the writers quoted between those I called 'poets mainly contributors' and those I thought of as 'holy writers' or 'saints'. The word 'saint' has many definitions. My own for this book is 'a writer who makes me aware of God's love'. I very much like Robert Frost's poem but dub him a 'contributor', whereas Thomas Traherne on so near a theme caught me when meditating on matters spiritual: he was writing specifically on the affairs of God.

But as the book progressed I found the distinctions blurred, the strands got entangled. After all, the plait was never going to be without its ravelling and unravelling and getting tied up in knots.

It doesn't matter. It's not important. All that matters is the sharing.

A Peck of Gold

Dust always blowing about the town,
Except when sea-fog laid it down,
And I was one of the children told
Some of the blowing dust was gold.

All the dust the wind blew high
Appeared like gold in the sunset sky,
But I was one of the children told
Some of the dust was really gold.

Such was life in the Golden Gate:
Gold dusted all we drank and ate,
And I was one of the children told,
'We all must eat our peck of gold.'

Robert Frost

Your enjoyment of the World is never right, till you so esteem it that everything in it, is more your treasure than a king's exchequer full of Gold and Silver. And that exchequer yours also in its place and service. Can you take too much joy in your Father's works? He is himself in everything. Some things are little on the outside, and rough and common, but I remember the time when the dust of the streets was as precious as Gold to my infant eyes, and now it is more precious to the eye of reason.
Thomas Traherne, *Centuries*

The corn was orient and immortal wheat which never could be reaped, nor was ever sown. I thought it had stood from everlasting to everlasting. The dust and stones of the street were as precious as gold: . . .

Century 3

Tall nettles cover up, as they have done
These many springs, the rusty harrow, the plough
Long worn out, and the roller made of stone:
Only the elm butt tops the nettles now.

This corner of the farmyard I like most:
As well as any bloom upon a flower
I like the dust on the nettles, never lost
Except to prove the sweetness of a shower.

       Edward Thomas

. . . I don't think that W.V., in spite of her confidence in my good faith, was quite convinced of the existence of those old forests of stone which, if men did not mar them, would blossom for centuries unchanged, though the hands that planted them had long been blown in dust about the world.

   William Canton, *A Child's Book of Saints*

   Dust's double dance
      is joy in death
  Inhaled by us
      in every breath.

  Yet as we live
      we barely know

  To dust we must
      as surely go.

  Oh! Am I dust?
      I touch this rose
  Of beauty's prize
  It looks at me
      with wondrous eyes:
      a petal falls.

> For several days
> > this heavenly rose
> Has caught my heart's
> > and eyes' repose
> And now to dust
> > the petal goes.
>
> But when to heaven
> > my soul ascends
> I'll know that heavenly
> > scent again.

I saw God in a point, that is to say, in mine understanding by which sight I saw that he is in all things.
> Julian of Norwich, *Revelations of Divine Love*

As a believer, I hold that God is creator of the world and so is present in every particle of his creation.
> John Dalrymple, *Simple Prayer*

The way human beings are made is that mystery stimulates our heart in a way that fully understood reality does not. This is especially true in the field of religion. There, mystery acts as a sure guide towards Truth.
> John Dalrymple, *Simple Prayer*

'A fitting epilogue for these sagas of courage,' wrote Elizabeth Basset at the end of the Preface to her anthology *Each in His Prison*, 'could be the words bequeathed by a German Jewish prisoner, which were found written on the walls of his cell in Cologne:

> 'I believe in the sun even when it is not shining.
> I believe in love even when I cannot feel it.
> I believe in God even when he is silent.'

This creed, which has inspired many people since it was first spread widely, also brings the thought that we should share what we believe. My life has been protected from the appalling suffering that I know has existed and still exists during the span of my twentieth-century life. My need is to accept the life that I am given, my own life, as it is, day by day. And now, having decided to spend time producing this book, I want to share (leaving aside others for the moment) this particular belief:

> I believe God is in the dust of the earth
> and tears of mankind
> I believe he keeps the tears bottled up
> to pour over the desert –
> and the desert will flower.

And I thank that unknown German Jew and hope that the gratitude of us all will be a part of his heaven.

The activity of sharing creates unity in the glorious growth of all creation into the Body of Christ. That which has been bottled up and left unshared will be revealed and used in the end for glory.

> Who look
> In steadiness, who gave among least things
> An under-sense of greatness, see the parts
> As parts, but with a feeling of the whole.

William Wordsworth, *The Prelude*

Julian of Norwich over 600 years ago shared her *Revelations of Divine Love*. She heard the Lord speaking to her and from her anchorite cell she wrote it all down. She says: 'We ought to rejoice in him, then, for what he shows and for what he hides! And if we humbly do this we shall experience great relief and earn eternal gratitude . . .' The writing took years. A scribe helped her and he added in a postscript: 'Beware of selecting only what you like, and leaving the rest . . .' Nevertheless, I must be forgiven for doing so. The quotations will surely leave the reader pining for more – for her whole book, indeed.

Her century was a time of great violence, sickness, plague, and upheaval on all sides. Though an anchorite, she was immersed in it. And now she is helping me and thousands of others to know the love of God. Is this not astounding?

Among the words she heard spoken to her were:

> It is known that I have done miracles here in the past, many, marvellous, estimable and great.
> What I did then, I do still, and shall continue to do.

Yes, she knew that mysteries are shown to us. The fact that they are mysteries does not invalidate them, for those who know about mystery discover the paradox: that such moments and understandings become the most real, important, vital certainties in their lives.

In *The Mystics of the Church*, Evelyn Underhill writes:

> Mysticism . . . is a life with an aim, and this aim
> is nothing less than the union of man's spirit
> with the very Heart of the Universe.

Throughout the centuries, thousands were able to testify to these things. And I myself can testify that God showed me a mystery at a moment of truth or revelation, call it what you will, that happened both in and out of time.

Richard Holloway, Bishop of Edinburgh, writes in *Seven to Flee, Seven to Follow*:

> The understanding mind, like the gentle author of Psalm 103, will know whereof we are made, remembering we are but dust; but I will also recognise that God has destined that dust for glory, and that it reflects the glory even now.

Yes, surely God is in and of and a part of and apart from the dust itself. He is its glory.

> God loves dust
> He must
> If you come to think about it
> And think of it
> you must
> God loves dust.
>
> He scooped it from his own
> exclusive power
> that made the universe
> and in his Hand
> made man.
> How else –
> could we ever understand
> what we cannot understand:
> God took the dust,
> yes, scooped it from
> His sunset-covered earth
> and wept
> tears of joy and sorrow.
>
> Was it from this mud and love
> He made us?

Try getting away from concepts only of lumpy clay; enjoy the story of Adam and Eve for its symbolism despite its loss of authenticity.

But dust is horrid, there's no getting away from it. And it is the last-seen stuff that gives unity to creation's dying where the decay of all things becomes simplified into a film of dirt which we cope with in order to restore the day to beauty and renewal.

Dust itself awaits resurrection. Blindly we shall see more and more into each speck's transformation. Yes, dust itself is ugly. And all we see as ugly *is* ugly except when God is revealing himself, and then it becomes beautiful. In this book, *that* is the moment of pure loveliness, the promise that all is made for glory, with every ugliness changed to radiancy, and a speck of dust showing us that the whole of God's creation is intrinsically glorious.

When I am totally empty of words, unable to speak to you and sunk into depression because of this failure, I listen to Julian. Over the six centuries she seems to sum it all up, to get it right.

> It is like this: when God was going to make man's body he took the dust of the earth, a matter which is a compound and collection of all sorts of material things and with it he made man's body. But when he would make man's soul he took nothing: he just made it. Thus is created nature rightly united with its Maker who is essential nature and uncreated; in other words, God. From which it follows that there can be nothing at all between God and man's soul.
> (Chapter 53)

Although there is no one whatsoever in this life who can get it completely right, in words or music or art, God gives us the saints who give us plenty of help if only we know how to use it. And sometimes they are themselves direct messengers of God's heart.

We, too, can hear his voice if only we can get into the

way of listening. And the fact is, that what we hear is simply meant for us, uniquely, you and me, every soul. God is trying to explain that it is in a seeming void that he is most at home. That is the greatest mystery within each individual life.

If, for example, you find as I do the numbers of stars in the galaxies, the numbers of fingers, toes and hairs of the world's heads simply too much for you, leave it to one side. That is God. He is beyond our minds. Accept the paradox: he loves every sparrow.

But from the huge expanses of time and distance comes this wisdom from India:

> When happy with vision and wisdom, he is master of his own inner life, his soul sublime set on high, then he is called a man in harmony. To him gold or stones or earth are one.
>
> Baghavad Gita

Yes, to gold and stones add dust. Are they not all as equal in the sight of the Creator as a forgotten child, or fly-covered infant, is equal to a prime minister, an archbishop or a pope? Jesus said so in his own day.

There will always be lots of books about God. None of them will explain or describe Him. How could that be? But the good ones will give clues and show us something about those who write from their hearts and minds and souls with love for Him. The fact is that everyone has that something within which springs in the first place from God. Somehow, somewhere, this stirring within is longing to break free and breathe and give expression to the love which inspired it. That is the work of the Holy Spirit.

Only a small fraction of all such thoughts and aspirations will find their way into words, and even fewer into words that get spelt out on paper. Yet fewer get themselves into extended form, and fewer still accepted by a publisher and on to shelves in bookshops and libraries. It is surprising there are so many books. It is the greatest surprise to me to write one (its future obscure), but a lovely surprise. And may the surprise in it be lovely for you and make something within you that has lain dormant, unexplored, spark into rapport.

This morning my next-door neighbour came over to ask if I could open a tin for her. Or was she a bit lonely? We chatted. Then she said: 'I was helped late last night on the radio. An Anglican priest was speaking and said his longing was that his hearers should have courage, gaiety and a quiet mind.'

Now that is what this is all about: living each day and finding, usually unexpectedly, just such messages of hope and faith and love.

There appeared on TV screens one evening a youngish, very rich German industrialist. He had been kidnapped and held hostage; he had endured terrible torture, and been chained and left in solitude. After his release and return to 'normal' life, he experienced a different distress of rejection both in his family and in his business. He then found, he said, unexpected release from so much pain and devastation by living in the present hour, even the moment, without going backwards and forwards in his mind, not allowing anxiety or worry to overcome him. He would say to himself: 'I am alive; getting up; eating breakfast; going out for a walk' and so on all day, until he found he could relish the present instant. He actually found joy itself. It was a memorable example of living in the present, a practice easily preached and hardly ever lived. It had become reality to him. And one could see it did not cut out the necessity to make plans for the future, which must be protected against not only the intrusion of fears and nightmares but also euphoria.

Here is Thomas Fuller's insight in *The Holy and the Profane*:

> He is a good time-server that improves the present for God's glory and his own salvation. Of all the extent of time, only the instant is what we can call 'ours'.

There is a moment in reading when you know you are hearing 'an answer to prayer'. Something is being told you, personally, that is exactly what you need at that hour, on that day. You are being given a 'lift', or maybe advice, or an indication of the direction to which you should turn. This is a common, expected experience when reading the Bible. It happens when a text leaves the page and becomes a guiding thought. It is different from enjoying a passage in a book, or a poem. It is more than intellectual; it speaks to the heart and soul.

How else can we hear the Word of God except through language? Or silence? And silence is part of language, of complementary value to that of the words, just as in music the rests and pauses are significant parts of the sound.

But even something as abstract as music depends upon ink on paper, written music, Italian directions, before it can be played. An artist's vision has to be conveyed by something as solid as canvas and pigment, brushes and palette.

The medieval family who took a day off and rode to the nearest cathedral had their ideas of God, no doubt. But they could not read, had no Bible or books in their cottage and were awed to see this House of God on earth and learn about God through the stained glass windows and carvings.

How much of nature herself have we seen through our TV screens? Programmes about the natural world can be as explosive to our imaginations as those windows in the cathedrals or churches. I have seen a mosquito born, a seal finding her baby among thousands of others and, oh, hundreds of other phenomena that I could never have known about without the dedicated researchers, photographers and presenters responsible for bringing such wondrous knowledge to us.

Then again it is the 'still life' painter who can open our eyes to the art of flower-arranging as something much more than simply putting flowers in a pot. And I do wonder whether Beethoven and Bruckner and Elgar and Vaughan Williams and all those who have written great music, together with the orchestras and soloists who perform it, have added to my appreciation of hearing the wind in the trees, the crashing of waves or the singing of the worms. Yes, they do sing and hum: that was on TV, too.

The Church is teaching us to be increasingly aware and absorbed into the all-ness of God in the world. There have been times when nature was preached as a snare and even a delusion! John Robinson pointed out in his book, *The Human Face of God*, that 'God changes not and God changes every day'. We wake up each morning into the process of evolution.

There are still lots of 'Sunday Christians', once-a-year, Midnight-Mass Christians, who departmentalise their ideas of God and find it difficult to understand about this Kingdom of God on earth. At one time it was assumed that scientists were at odds with Christianity – or any religious faith – but this is no longer so, and we can be excited about this change. Loving God is to see more and more into everything around us.

There's a game for infants in which the leader puts them into a circle and pushes them away until they cannot touch or reach each other. 'Shut your eyes now,' says the leader, 'and imagine that I am Jesus, and you are going to take a step towards me. Stretch out your arms. OK? Now open your eyes! You see? You can touch your next-door friend. Now shut your eyes again.' This can be taken a step further. The children are now touching Jesus, so you say: 'Close your eyes again! Now, very, very quiet; listen very carefully. Jesus is going to whisper something.' Jesus whispers: 'I love you!' Then you say: 'Open your eyes, run about the room, clap, jump, skip and shout: Jesus loves me!' (Keep control. Only allow this for a short time, and be ready to sing immediately a favourite hymn or song that they know very well and love singing.)

When the children have done this a few times, they always want to play it again. That's really what life is all about.

Well, we won't actually play this game! We would look ridiculous and feel ridiculous; we are not children, and some of us are beyond skipping and dancing. But maybe deep down we wish we could, we wish we could be children again, sometimes, just for a while. We are children at heart. That is what Jesus means when he says: 'Let the children come to me.' Drop the barriers and the rationalisations and the fears. Simply: 'Come to me!'

Perhaps we can be helped to cope with the huge expanses of knowledge that have been opened up in the last fifty years if we consider the wisdom that goes back thousands of years – even to the heart of the earliest Man. (And Woman, of course!)

That great saying of Ronnie, aged seven, is one to remember. He said: 'I love everybody and everything, even ants. God made ants to be loved not trodden on.'

Francis Thompson wrote of the child:

> The universe is his, his box of toys. He dabbles his fingers in the day-fall. He is gold-dusty with tumbling among the stars.

In conversation recently a friend enjoyed describing a young couple who had gone to the curate for a wedding interview. They said: 'We are not church-goers, but he was ever so nice, 'e wouldn't 'ave trod on a centipede!' Perhaps the curate was a modern prophet who in his person foretold the last days when 'the lion shall lie down with the lamb'.

But the glory is God's, as Pascal saw when he wrote from God's view-point:

> Let the glory be mine and not yours, O worm and dust.

The worm and the dust will be transformed.

> O ye dust and ashes bless ye the Lord.
> Praise him and magnify him for ever.

P.A. Sveeggen prayed:

> Though I am but dust, I pray,
> Before God standing.

And God said . . . I will remember my covenant which is between me and you and every living creature.

> Genesis 9.12-15

> Heavenly Father, Heavenly Mother
> We long for happiness
> But lead us beyond happiness
> To that joy which nothing can
> take away.
>
> Bp. R. Harris, *The Pursuit of Happiness*

The special moment I want to share was a mystery, and that means something paradoxical, both simple and profound. The idea of mixing it in with an anthology and comments on the subject of dust is to make the ripples widen, like throwing it as a pebble into a still lake. Or, if you prefer, like wrapping it carefully into a parcel, marked 'fragile'. I wanted to surround myself with encouragements, for writing is a lonely occupation. You can skip on to Part II, if you prefer to know now what happened, and come back later. But I would rather you waited.

I have delved a little among the poets. It would have been possible to turn also to the scientists.

The whole question of what God was wanting me to understand covers a lifetime of prayer and its meaning. 'And now we only see darkly.'

For no one can give a name to God, who is too great for words; if anyone claims to say that it is possible to do so, he must be suffering from an incurable madness.

St Justin Martyr

Leon Bloy wrote: 'When we speak lovingly of God all words are like blinded lions seeking a spring in the desert.'

I chose the plait concept only to emphasise that we are all responsible for each other, we are interwoven. Think, for example, of one letter through the post:

>The person who wrote it,
>posted it
>and the postman.
>The sorters
>the train and its engineers, electricians and the
>   driver.
>Who designed the stamp?
>Printed it?

Made the dyes . . .
And the paper and envelope, where did they
come from?
The pen that was used . . .
Shopkeepers . . .
and then you read it!

Anything autobiographical must radiate circles interlocking and meshing to create a whole, depending on the sort of cog wheel we are ourselves.

I know almost nothing of solitude and yet it is an unknown solitary German Jew that gave me the push to get typing. And the fact is, plainly, that my subject *Dust Glorified* is far beyond words.

The name of Yahweh should not be pronounced. The name of God is too wondrous to be spoken. The Tibetan monks know this, as they sit in their lotus positions intoning over and over and over again:

Aum . . . Aah . . . Oom

And over again:

Aum . . . Aah . . . Oom

In the East there is this word for wordlessness: *Aum*. It becomes a humming sound of rounded perfection, the sound of unutterable devotion, the wordless offering of self to God, dependent on His will.

God is a word that we should never be asked to write or speak. It is beyond language as those monks know. But we use it a lot. It is plaited firmly into life. We could not get on without it. We even blaspheme – continually – 'O God!', 'Christ!'

To say Thou art God, without knowing what the Thou means – of what use is it? God is a name only except we know God.

George Macdonald, *The Temptation in the Wilderness*

'O God!' I cried and that was all. But what are the prayers of the whole universe more than expansions of that one cry? It is not what God can give us, but God we want.

George Macdonald, *Wilfred Cumbermead*

But remember, Lord, that we are dust, and that of dust thou hast made man; and he was lost and is found. Nor could he of himself do this, because he whom I so loved, saying this through the in-breathing of Thy Inspiration, was of the same dust.

St Augustine, *Confessions*, XXX/45

There are two ways of bringing into communion
The diversity of particular gifts:
The love of sharing
And the sharing of love.
Thus the particular gift becomes common
To him who has it and to him who has it not:
He who has it
Communicates it by sharing,
He who has it not
Participates by communion.

Baldwin of Ford, Archbishop of Canterbury, died 1190

From Dust I rise
> And out of Nothing now awake;
These brighter Regions which salute mine Eyes
> A Gift from God I take:
The Earth, the Seas, the Light, the lofty Skies,
The Sun and Stars are mine; if these I prize.

A stranger here
Strange things doth meet, strange glory see,
Strange Treasures lodg'd in the fair World appear,
> Strange all and New to me:
But that they *mine* should be who Nothing was,
That Strangest is of all; yet brought to pass.

> Thomas Traherne, *Centuries*

This last poem was chosen by Cecil Day Lewis as the first poem in a collection under the title *A Lasting Joy*. I was over the moon to find this book years later in the local library. (And how many others shared it?) Plaiting the poem in here I hope to pass on my joy.

What about the expression 'over the moon'? We all use it and know what we mean, but originally it belonged to the secret language of the Glynne sisters. Catherine Glynne married William Gladstone. Slowly others shared it; their glossary became fashionable in a widening circle. Now it even appears in the *Concise Oxford Dictionary*.

> The history of a language . . . lies in its dust.

> Philip Howard,
> article in *The Times*, 30 August 1988

Language is of such complexity that a history can be written about each word. Yet with all the world's languages and dialects at our command there are some experiences that we cannot put into words. We say: 'I can't find a word for it. There are no words to describe it.' Both language and silence are amazing.

This book is only concerned with one insight – that dust became glory. And (if you haven't already skipped ahead and back) my reason for writing around the incident, making this plait or parcel of it, putting off describing it, is to allow it to permeate a general attitude towards other everyday events and words.

I have chosen four words which we use continually to give an example of why words can be limiting when describing any religious experience. Neither 'dust' nor 'glory' is an easy concept, but neither are 'joy', 'peace', 'love' and 'endurance'.

So here are four memory flash-backs which brought each of these words into a beam of significance for me personally.

Joy

The word crops up in sermons, hymns and our everyday talk. It is the heart's beat of our experience of God whether we acknowledge this or not. Here is how I heard it in a sermon remembered now nearly sixty years later.

I was fifteen years old, sitting in the pew at Evensong on a hot summer evening in All Saints, West Alvington, in the South Hams (Devon). I did not always go to Evensong; sometimes I played tennis at the Squire's stately home, or sat by the fire at home. It was expected that we would attend Matins at 11.00a.m., and also, when confirmed, get up early and go to Holy Communion at 8.00a.m. But my father was the parson, and sometimes I felt compelled to accompany him on the walk from our beautiful vicarage up the lane to the last service of the day. He was lonely. And to preach two sermons each Sunday, week after week, year after year, required much perseverance, endurance even. Once there, however, in church, it was no hardship for me after all; the atmosphere inside was totally heart-warming. It was the service to which the 'village' turned out. The 'gentry' tended to stay at home to entertain. My father was 'gentry', carrying on a Victorian tradition in the role of the youngest son. In those 'thirties' years, the rumblings about the need for a revolution in the class system went unheeded.

In the church that summer evening, where an atmosphere of tranquillity prevailed, Sunday hats were on; there had been a slight stir of interest around the notices of fête, or outing, or care for the sick; hymns were being sung with fervour in a lusty Devonian accent. What would parson be on about in the sermon tonight? It was *Joy*. And although he must have preached well over 1,000 sermons in that church, I never heard him repeat what he said then.

J stood for Jesus, O for others, and Y for yourself. That was the order. Y must be very much the last. He filled out the lovely message for ten to fifteen minutes to a lulled congregation with their eye on old Jefferies, who would be waiting for his cue to pump the organ for the last hymn.

And for me the sermon had gone home – although I was unlikely to discuss such a moving experience.

But vicarage children develop their own sort of irreverence. It became a joke, of course. When the deck-chairs needed to be brought in, we would shout 'O for others'. Many tiresome domestic jobs were open to the same call. Beneath trivialities one was learning to grow out of the early childhood Jesus who was just a far-distant bearded man in white robes illustrated in our detailed picture book, and into the unseen Master and Lord who had been a Friend for Little Children. We said our prayers to Him night and morning on our knees by

Dust

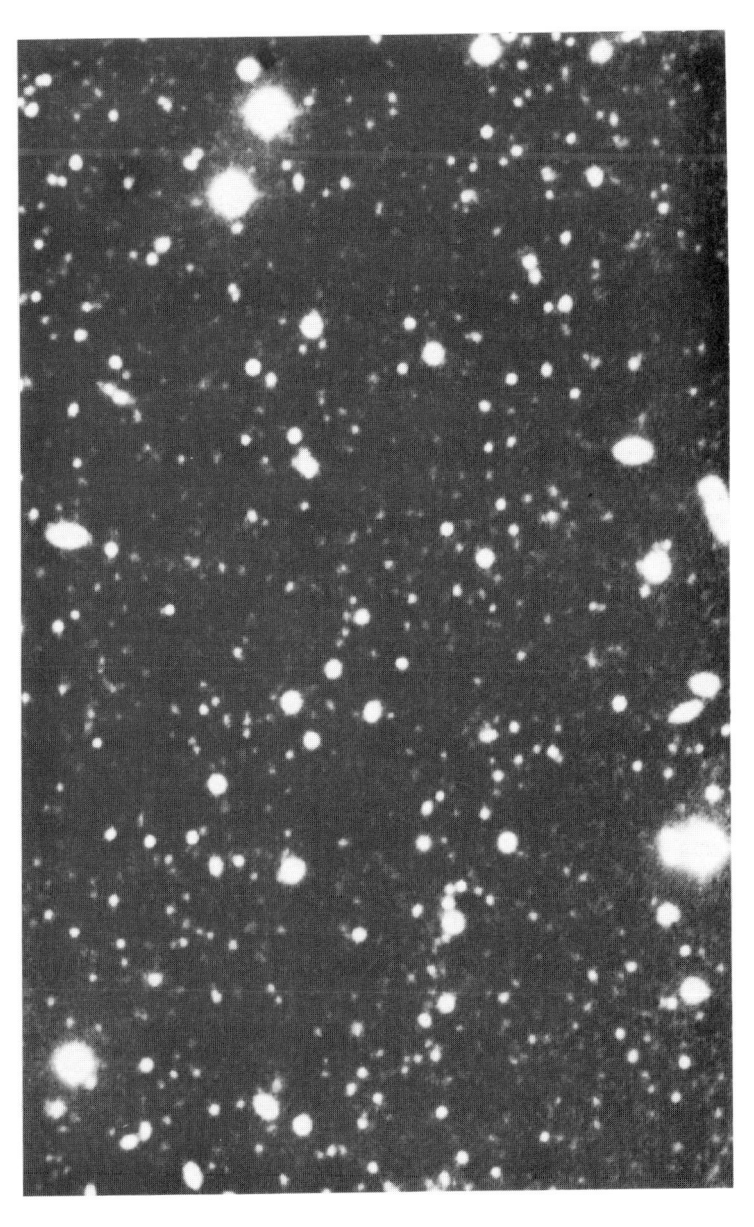

Stars – see the Appendix

bedside. And what do I not owe to that? But as we grew into adolescence it was a 'double-shuffle' to keep strongly to one's faith and at the same time throw off parental beliefs: to take on one's own. There was a general feeling that, if you were a vicarage child, you were bound to become a 'baddy' or a 'goody', and that it was almost impossible to keep going somewhere in between.

I have written all that to explain what a big change it was in my thinking much later on in life to find that a better way towards living the Christian faith was – in learning about love – first to love yourself. Or, as Teilhard de Chardin put it:

> If a man is to be fully himself and fully living, he must (1) be centred on himself, (2) be 'de-centred' upon the other, (3) 'be super-centred' upon a being greater than himself.

I have discussed and heard this discussed in many circles and among many friends. It involves a much greater change than a few sentences might imply.

So now we see the importance of loving ourselves, rightly understood, in order to reach an inner peace; not forever 'escaping', making demands on others, or seeking ego-trips. And these ego-trips can be very complex and far-roaming. Know yourself? Nothing so new about that, some may say. But the quite remarkable burgeoning of counsellors and healing services are proof, if one were needed, of this need. Not until some degree of serenity and integration is reached is one able to be of use to others. Then one finds that it is in giving and receiving that love really grows. Or, rather, it will be in coming to terms with that which we find disturbing, difficult, embittering, in our own lives, that we are able to learn love and forgiving and forgiveness. So we come to Jesus through others and not in isolation or denigration of ourselves.

It is interesting to reflect that the disaster of Aberfan was the first national occasion when the Government realised the necessity of setting up immediate counselling services, so that the bereaved and stunned could find someone to talk to. It is still a comparatively new social policy, although so obviously common sense.

Paul wrote to the early Christians in Rome: 'with the joyful be joyful, and mourn with the mourners' (Romans 12.15, NEB). Some days you need to move between one and the other!

> Joy & Woe are woven fine,
> A Clothing for the Soul divine;
>
> William Blake, 'Auguries of Innocence'

A prayer by Martin Israel:

> May I have the sensitivity, Lord, to be of comfort to my suffering neighbour by giving my very essence to relieve the pain and set the tortured mind at rest. May I have the inner joy to relish another's good fortune and to add to its celebration.

So there are some words that you long to use for the first time every time you use them. Such a word is *Joy*.

There is more to being 'surprised by joy' than anything a sermon can contain – more than all the books and poems in the world can show.

The Abba Moses asked the Abba Silvanus, Can a man everyday make a beginning of the good life? The Abba Silvanus answered him, If he be diligent, he can every day and every hour begin the new life anew.

Love and Peace

> Then I saw God to be our true peace, when we are anything but peaceful and who always works to bring us to everlasting peace.
>
> Julian, *Revelations of Divine Love*, 49

An African priest was being interviewed by Pauline Webb in Harare, Zimbabwe, at the end of an important World Churches Conference there. At the close of a long interview he was asked: 'What would you like to say, finally, to the millions watching this programme? What is your final message?' He said: 'It can all be summed up in two words – love and peace.' Christ was born to be love in the world and peace. He was love and peace. He is love and peace. He will, as love and peace, come again.

But my task is not to write about love and peace, or even hope, but to try to face up to dust . . .

Dust is the most precious, important thing about our lives. It is life. We are made of dust, we go to dust. That's all. That's it. Praise the Lord!

It means the end of all things has a beginning. God is dust because he took upon Himself His own nature to make us in His image. From dust he created the universe. Actually Something Other, beyond our understanding!

And so, dust is also *Love*.

Dust is darkness, terror and despair. It chokes. It blots out all beauty. It stinks. It repels. Dust is all the horror of evil. It means waste and pain, the slow destruction of things. And because God is a great Being of paradox and surprises – dust is glory.

What does this mean?

Does it suggest the following? There is no possibility for you to contemplate God in all His peace and love and infinite wisdom unless, until, you have contemplated the darkness and sufferings of the world we live in. Unless you have let the starving Ethiopians, the drowning Indians, the homeless Britons, the skeletons of Auschwitz, and the sorrows of your next-door neighbour into your soul.

When you can carry a battered baby in your heart's warm heaviness, wash the frozen feet of a dirty tramp, kiss a leper or simply remove nits from a child's hair, you can begin to laugh with the laughter of the saints. 'Rejoice again, I say, rejoice.' To look the other way – to leave someone else to empty the hoover bag, tip out the refuse – won't do. It simply won't do.

Come, let us contemplate dust – without fear or disgust. Of course, I am not so daft as to think we shall any of us be a Saint Francis or Mother Theresa of Calcutta or the Good Samaritan. They are suns as we are glow-worms. But we may glow in the dark, if we are willing to try.

God is only asking us to respond in whatever way we are able. Maybe it is only washing up the supper things.

But even if we are at the sink, we must hang on to a vision. Our own personal vision of something good ahead, something worth striving for, some goal to achieve. 'Where there is no vision the people perish' (Proverbs 18).

> This is true
> What is your vision?
> Mine?
> Does it come in the countless little things?
> Butterfly wings?
> Or was it in that unforgettable sunset?
> (Between Totnes and Kingsbridge)
> Was it that moment in church
> when God took your heart and hand?
> A blessing?

>
> Or in the street?
> Understand?
> We must want our visions –
> beyond our day-dreams
> beyond our longings,
> beyond hope.
> A vision of utterly complete
> fulfilment of ourselves
> and the whole world – in God.

Bishop Gilpin took the same text on some grand occasion in the great parish church of Kingston on Thames. I remember the text but not the sermon. I remember (probably to my shame) being critical of the sermon, laughing a bit. Did he overdo it? Or was it me, flat, critical, without response, without my own vision?

Dust that we are, what recompense is it even to give our whole poor selves to Him?

> St Bernard of Clairvaux on the Love of God

We give ourselves to God through love for our neighbour, at work, travelling, in hospital, visiting, shopping, wherever.

If we are at a loss for some voluntary work to do, it is well to bear in mind there is a huge number of charities registered in this country to date. That should give some idea of the choice of work there is around!

There is no way out unless we want to escape altogether, which has great attractions. I should know. Just at the moment I am longing to escape from writing to you about dust.

I hoped that summoning up and weaving the saints into the plait would strengthen and encourage me, but sometimes the effect is quite otherwise; I feel intimidated in their company. Especially when I come across such a paragraph as this, from *The Go-Between God* by John V. Taylor:

> In any case there have always been the saints. Perhaps these 'little Christs' are the fruit which proves the dry branches are still part of the true Vine. And how miraculously they have reflected his likeness in all their variety! Francis of Assisi and Teresa of Avila, Nicholas Ferrar and George Fox, Tikhon of Veronezh and the Curé d'Ars, Edward Wilson, explorer of the Antarctic, and Apolo Kivebulaya, apostle to the pygmies, Simone Weil, Dag Hammarskjöld and Martin Luther King – across the centuries and the different traditions, they show an astonishing family likeness, recognisable in the same ardent awareness, piercing discernment, defiant nonconformity and total self-abandonment that we have noted in Jesus.

But to be intimidated in their company? That is absurd. A complete misunderstanding. Fortunately there is no question of comparison, or some subtle (and evil) form of competitiveness. The saints are there to help us. We can claim their help. We can trust them to help us. It is one of the very nastiest forms of pride that says: 'I am not good enough for this or that . . .'

Of course we are not good enough. Pascal got it right, we are worms and dust. And God loves us *just as we are*.

Endurance

A dear old widow in the Norfolk village of Trunch gave me a little Victorian book. I knew it had been precious to her for a long time, and was moved by her generosity.

But more than that, I guessed she wanted me to share something written in it. She lived alone in Chapel Lane and I treasured the time we spent together in her garden. After all these years I have forgotten her name and feel sad about that. But I am also ashamed to say that I did not read the book straight away; I put it away for 'another day'. The book was *Above the Mists* by George Howard Williams DD. The author was the Most Reverend the Bishop of St Andrews, Primus of the Episcopal Church in Scotland. It was published at the time of his death in 1911, price 1/6d, in the Gem series.

Trying ruthlessly to reduce my possessions, I decided to pass it on to Michael Hare Duke, the present Bishop of St Andrews, as a Christmas present. But before doing so I sat down to read it and found it was indeed a 'gem' and spoke to me of encouragement, enlightenment and help at hand. On page 71 it reads:

> All the saints of God would tell you the same thing. There have been periods when the Spirit – for years maybe seemed to be cleaving to the dust; when there seemed no power of realising God's presence . . . very often the trials that come upon us and the sorrows which we have to bear have nothing to do with our own sins, nor, except indirectly, with our own spiritual discipline. We pray for our children; we pray for those whom we love; and the answer comes through bankruptcy, a broken heart, an open grave, a desolated home. We know not what it means . . . Very often your heaviest trials will fall upon you not for your own sin, but in virtue of that glorious office into which you have been baptised, the office of God's prophet . . .
> Endurance; the last great offering of ourself, when work, even intercession, are past.

'When the spirit . . . seemed to be cleaving to the dust.'

Was the author not steeped in the Psalms himself?

> Rouse yourself O Lord why do you sleep?
> Awake do not cast us off for ever.
> Why do you hide your face:
> And forget our misery and affliction?
> Our souls are bowed to the dust:
> Our bellies cleave to the ground.
> Arise O Lord to help us;
> And redeem us for your mercy's sake.
>
> Psalm 44.23-26, NEB

> I am humbled to the dust:
> > O give me life according to your word.
> If I examine my ways:
> > Surely you will answer me; O teach me
> > your statutes!
> Make me understand the way of your precepts:
> > and I shall meditate on your marvellous
> > > works.
>
> Psalm 119.25-27, NEB

Laurens van der Post has a sentence for this in his lovely book *The Praying Mantis*, a story of love as shown in the life of Hans Taaibosche of *The Lost Tribe of the Kalahari Desert* and the American woman who dreamed of Mantis:

> And I knew as never before that there was no greater beauty (in my own round of life on earth) possible in nature or man than that of the uncared for and rejected, rediscovered and redeemed for growth through hope.

So I asked a passing ancient clergyman: 'What would

you say to me if you knew I was writing a book about dust?' 'Good Heavens!' he said, and his mind leapt to a sad episode of the Second World War. He told me of a young airman 'blown to smithereens in the air . . .'

And I remembered the bomb that missed me by a few yards and utterly obliterated the jewellery shop that I had just visited to collect a mended clock. In less than a minute it was all rubble and a cloud of choking dust, old 'Ticker' Lewis and his wife killed. I might have been dust myself now.

But I am not. And I still want to postpone coming to the heart of the matter – of why I am writing.

I want us to turn our minds to the connection between dust and the stars and the clocks, and to cogitate a little while longer on such things, in order to glimpse the extent of this End and Beginning of things (in creation), the Alpha and Omega of God.

> Dust in sunlight and memory in corners
> Wait . . .
>
> T.S. Eliot, 'A Song for Simeon'

'Ashes to ashes and dust to dust' is not merely a religious and philosophical doctrine but a scientific truth of such profundity that it should be engraved over the entrance to every Faculty of Medicine throughout the world.

> Peter Tompkins & Christopher Bird,
> *The Secret Life of Plants*

The Gift of Oneself by Joseph Shryver is a very special book and it seems to be out of print. Here are two extracts from the section headed 'God works wonders in the soul that is surrendered to His action'.

The drop of dew, the speck of dust, the insect hidden in the grass, present insoluble problems to the student . . .

The smallest insect hidden under a leaf has its destiny as well as has the deer in the forest; the grain of dust floating in the air has its purpose as well as have the measureless globes that traverse space; the lowliest mortal, the unknown slave wandering in the heart of the desert, has his end to attain as well as the monarch presiding over the destinies of the world.

> If Chance can dance the dust afar
>   in myriad motions to a star,
> If Chance can mould with pollen gold
>   the silken seeds where lilies are,
> If Chance one daisy can enfold
>   then God the hand of Chance must hold.

> from *Short Prayers for the Long Day*
> compiled by Giles & Melville Harcourt

'Was it chance?' Dr John Houghton, Director of the Meteorological Office, was giving his talk on *This Is the Day* (BBC Radio 4, 30 September 1990). 'Was it chance that among 1,000 x 1,000,000 stars of our own galaxy (there are lots of other galaxies) the planet earth was where Jesus was born?'

Children often know. Watch them when they sing 'Away in a Manger', or:

> All things bright and beautiful
> All creatures great and small
> All things wise and wonderful
> Our Lord God made them all.

And watch them even more carefully, especially if they have never been taught a thing about it, how they sing: 'Still, still, Jesus is here.'

Turning from children to one of the most eminent physicists of our time, Professor Stephen Hawking, we read in the last paragraph of his book, *A Brief History of Time: From the Big Bang to Black Holes*:

> However, if we do discover a complete theory, it should in time be understandable in broad principle by everyone, not just a few scientists. Then we shall all, philosophers, scientists and just ordinary people, be able to take part in the discussion of the question of why it is that we and the universe exist. If we find the answer to that, it would be the ultimate triumph of human reason for then we would know the mind of God.

I tried to read this book, without understanding much of it. But I shall never forget the TV programme on 17 October 1983 from Cambridge, when, surrounded by his admiring students, he was discussing these issues, the Quantum Theory and so on, illustrated by equations on the board that looked like incomprehensible hieroglyphics but must have meant something to those who study with him. (John Polkinghorne has written *The Way God Is* to try to make this intelligible to those like me.) The great unforgettable moment was right at the end of the programme when he was asked to sum it all up and talk of the future. He looked, as some great seer of all mysteries, and, to my utter surprise, said:

> Dust to dust, and ashes to ashes, and singularity to singularity.

So dust forms the stars! Is Halley's comet a solid mass or made up of dust? That is what the eminent astronomers were discussing – right there – in front of the cameras during that famous wait, one 1988 evening, watching for the probe. Their excitement intense. And ours – sharing theirs. What a privilege! My ignorance infected with their knowledge and enthusiasm. What an occasion!

'Stars are children of dust,' one said in passing. He might have said 'children of quarks and gluons' for all I would comprehend, so ignorant am I of the galaxies, of the sky at night. But the expression 'children of dust' hit me like a sledge-hammer. Had I not read a book with that title a few years back? Indeed, it was an unforgettable book, though I had forgotten the name of the wonderful girl who wrote it. She had been struck at the age of fifteen with a TV news item about Vietnam, just as the war was ending, when the Americans were leaving and chaos reigned. She saved up her pocket money. From that moment she was determined to get there – as a nurse if possible – but get there. And she did. And then worked with street children, among others. She visited the prisons, and she did the most amazing things with compassion but also with laughter and without fear. She called her book *Children of Dust* because that was the name that the children were given as they were swept up and around the streets. Once a week a police van did a special sweep, taking them to prison. There they were, left in a large concrete room with one hole in the centre for their needs. The obscenity of what this chapter of her book describes has haunted me for years. Today, ten years later, the newspaper has statistics of all these children around the world. There are 14 million of them at this time, and the police are shooting them now, like rats.

When I put this sheet of paper in the typewriter, I intended to write a page about dew-drops and their sparkle of beauty in the autumn sunrise suspended on the spider's web!

A few weeks ago it was another misery. I watched thousands fighting, dying even, for a drop of water in the desert of Jordan, and I went upstairs to have a bath.

No wonder we need a widening comprehension to face our problems of pain. To see things within the perspective of eternity.

O God! And you know it all, you are there in them all, you are every child, every drop of dew, every speck of dust. What was it you said to Abraham?

> I will make your descendants as the dust of the earth; so that if one can count the dust of the earth, your descendants also can be counted.
> Arise, walk through the length and the breadth of the land, for I will give it you. (Genesis 13.16-17)

Much later on in Abraham's life, there came that most terrible request from God: 'Take your son, your only son Isaac, whom you love . . . and offer him there as a burnt offering . . .' (Genesis 22.2).

What can we believe in response to this story? Only that God did the same himself for our sake. But I cannot write of these great mysteries – others preach their sermons, write their commentaries. But I do read on and find that, having tested Abraham to the uttermost, God speaks to Abraham again:

> I will indeed bless you, and I will multiply your descendants as the stars of heaven and as the sand which is on the seashore. (Genesis 22.17)

God seems to have got muddled up between dust and sand and stars himself! Unless they are the same.

Of all William Blake's immense output of writing, one verse – the opening lines of 'Auguries of Innocence' – has hit the headlines:

> To see a World in a Grain of Sand
>   And a Heaven in a Wild Flower,
> Hold Infinity in the palm of your hand

And Eternity in an hour.

So where am I now?

In my imagination on Trimingham beach stranded by the hard work of communication, longing to give up and search for pebbles. But time is short in a life-span, and there is not a day to waste. Dust has lived in a long hour, rubbed from a living day, thrown away to earth from which life began. From whatever it once was it has become the earth from which the turnip will grow. The turnip in today's stew. So Miss T?

> It's a very odd thing
> As odd as can be
> That whatever Miss T eats
> Turns into Miss T;
> Porridge and apples,
> Mince, muffins and mutton,
> Jam, junket, jumbles –
> Not a rap, not a button
> It matters; the moment
> They're out of her plate,
> Though shared by Miss Butcher
> And sour Mr Bate;
> Tiny and cheerful,
> And neat as can be,
> Whatever Miss T eats
> Turns into Miss T.
>
> Walter de la Mare, *Peacock Pie*

But what did you think, feel, when as a child you had your first sighting of dust? I remember mine: I was in my parents' bedroom, sitting on the floor. There, right around me, were these horrors. I was appalled. I tried not to breathe. I ran away into the dark and tried to forget.

We can move from revulsion to ecstasy. Once I had many thoughts about the wonder of cow-pats, their use as fuel, for thatching and so on. Of course, when dried out. The splosh, splosh is hardly attractive. And yet, I met a friend and we had a conversation about cow-pats! She said: 'You know, I loved them when I was a child. I was brought up on a farm and when they were covered in flies I used to jump on them and scream with delight when all the flies flew away.' You never know! The Africans use them to build and thatch and burn. Sometimes they polish them before use.

> Do not select: at God's command the angels bring
> A load of dung as lief as rest themselves and sing.
>
> Angelus Silesius

In the First World War it was discovered that wounded soldiers left out in the field were better off if maggots settled on their wounds and ate the damaged skin and kept the wound clean.

Cobwebs were used for centuries to bind cuts and wounds. And mouldy bread was made into compresses for poisoned fingers etc. So what repels can also heal. Dust becomes resurrection's delight. Could it be that we see dust as a symbol not of death but of love indestructible, forever renewable, moving towards a love enfolding?

So let love return to end this rambling introduction for the clarity of what is to come. And here is George Herbert's poem that has transformed many hearts and minds, notably having a profound influence on the philosophical mind of Simone Weil (as described in *Wait on God, Letters of Farewell*).

Love (III)

Love bade me welcome; yet my soul drew back,
    Guiltie of dust and sinne.
But quick-ey'd Love, observing me grow slack
    From my first entrance in,
Drew nearer to me, sweetly questioning,
    If I lack'd any thing.

A guest, I answer'd, worthy to be here:
    Love said, You shall be he.
I the unkinde, ungratefull? Ah my deare,
    I cannot look on thee.
Love took my hand, and smiling did reply,
    Who made the eyes but I?

Truth Lord, but I have marr'd them: let my shame
    Go where it doth deserve.
And know you not, sayes Love, who bore the
                               blame?
    My deare, then I will serve.
You must sit down, sayes Love, and taste my meat:
    So I did sit and eat.

PART II

This Speck of Dust Glorified

Every visible and invisible creature is a theophany or appearance of God.
> John Scotus Erigena

He clothed the hills with a rainbow to tell me His goodness would not fail, and so I had faith.
> Anon.

For God is in the man, and God is in everything. And by the grace of God I hope that anyone who looks at it in this way will be taught aright, and greatly comforted if need be.

> Julian of Norwich, *Revelations of Divine Love*

When the light of sense goes out, but with a flash that has reveal'd the invisible world.
> William Wordsworth

There was no delusion in the matter; it was no nebulous ecstasy, but a state of transcendant wonder, associated with absolute clearness of mind.

> Alfred, Lord Tennyson

> Stand amaz'd ye heavens at this!
> See the Lord of earth and skies
> Humbled to the dust he is
> And in a manger lies.
>
> Charles Wesley

This is what happened.

I wrote it down at the time, after cycling back to Dockhead in Bermondsey. I put it in an envelope, stuck it down, and put it in my Bible. There it stays.

Years later I wrote it out again for a godchild with a letter. This too survives, in a drawer, unposted.

Forty years on I wrote it again, intending a book, but it got abandoned and stays in a cardboard box in the attic.

This time I find all three versions read almost word for word the same, although I did not copy them one from another. This version is the one intended for the god-daughter, and the letter that might have gone with it.

Dear June,

Are you yet old enough to imagine what it is like when something happens . . . and this something is just as vivid in your experience so many years later?

It astounds me because of all the other things that have happened, more or less remembered, forgotten. How do these memories live? What feeds them? Where do the starved ones go? At the time, of course, you say to yourself: I will never forget – I will remember that all my life.

But with what guarantee? I would love to tell you a fraction of the memory of a second. I only tell you now because it has survived the test of time's sifting; such events, not uncommonly, go on living in our present although, we now see darkly, they belong to Eternity.

I bicycled to St George's Church on a cotton dress day, lovely sunshine, and propped the bike against the warm stone wall.

It was like a tomb inside, dark and intensely chilly. Even when my eyes were accustomed it seemed forbidding. My steps echoed. I went through to the Blessed Sacrament Chapel which was more welcoming, and waited for the priest. I had come for my confession, not the easiest time, waiting. (All right afterwards – wonderful then.)

I tried to roam over the guilts and fears, the selfish messes, impatience, criticism – you can't really ever explain what all that is like. Sin was not such an avoided word then, and there were sorts of formulae, never adequate, but a help. In the end only the absolution mattered and being openly sorry, truly sorry. I was that. And I was ready to go through with it. But he never came. In all the years that has happened only twice, to be forgotten. I couldn't help being rather relieved, but it didn't seem right to be so glad. I prayed and said how sorry I was and uninhibitedly emptied my heart – perhaps more fully than I could have done to the priest – but don't get me wrong, it is better done properly. But I was forgiven and the happiness flooded over and strength came back. It is the incredible experience of real joy. So, I began to think about glory.

There's got to be glory, I thought. An ugly word – got. How, got to be glory? Let there be glory, let there be light, let the glory shine, and the light shine, that glory be shown.

Who is the Lord of Hosts? He is the King of Glory. Glory is of God, glory is God.

There's got to be glory. Meaning? Obtained? Found? Acquired? Glory does not exist of itself. Glory is only in God. Glory is God and God is glory.

There's got to be glory. Where? On our face? In our

work, as we bike through the streets, sit beside old gran, help the children play? We can be patient, perhaps, laugh, cry, hold the fearful hand, take a frail arm. But how shall there be glory? 'How, O God . . .' I tried to pray.

Before I could still my mind, empty it, wait (although I had done a lot of waiting by then), I looked up and saw a beam from the sun shining through the huge church. Another smaller beam was right beside me. In this the dust specks were all floating with extraordinary purpose and slowness. As though they were playing galaxies, never touching each other.

It was fascinating. They appeared and disappeared into the sun, shining like stars, it was like glimpsing a mobile terrestrial calm, and all just close in front of my eyes.

Then, one speck, rather larger than most, hovered and suspended itself, like a haloed pin's head. It grew to the size of a penny, and time became suspended with it. In this speck of dust I saw quite clearly, as if I had been standing before a masterpiece in an art gallery, a picture of the Madonna and Child.

It was not unusual in comparison with the many that I had studied for years, but definitely I had never seen it before. It was vivid, unique and very beautiful.

As suddenly, it was gone, caught away, and dancing with the others in this constant choreographic theme. This microscopic and yet quite large sight left me quite calm, until a moment later when I thought: 'Where was I?' And I remembered as if from a long while before: of course I was thinking of glory.

And then, Glory Be, my heart jumped. Then I was shaken, as if a car had all but knocked me off the pavement. Was I thinking of glory? And here in the speck of dust glory showed itself to me. Glory in dust, or dust in glory? This is all true. How could it not be? Impossible to invent, happening once, there, at a special moment, in an actual place and becoming a jewel in memory's treasure trove: glory revealed in dust! Was God showing me a truth about glory? Dust and ashes. What was contained in the dust? From where and to where was it travelling?

Julian says: 'In short, everything owes its existence to the love of God' (*Revelations of Divine Love*).

> Even the dust, and what is dust, what long life is it leading? Shall we know God in every speck of dust?

The incarnation of Jesus Christ is in all creation. As we read in Genesis:

> Then the Lord God formed a man from the dust of the ground and breathed into his nostrils the breath of life. Thus the man became a living creature. (2.7)

> . . . dust you are, to dust you shall return. (3.19)

> Though earth and moon were gone,
>   And suns and universes ceased to be,
> And Thou wert left alone,
>   Every existence would exist in Thee.
>
> Emily Brontë, 'Last Lines'

It was at this time that our Lord showed me spiritually how intimately he loves us. I saw that he is everything that we know to be good and helpful. In his love he clothes us, enfolds and embraces us; that tender love completely surrounds us, never to leave us. As I saw it he is everything that is good. And he showed me more

... God showed me too the pleasure it gives him when a simple soul comes to him, openly, sincerely and genuinely.

> Julian of Norwich, *Revelations of Divine Love*

> Nor ever rest, nor ever lie
> Till beyond thinking, out of view
> One mote of all the dust that's I
> Shall meet one atom that was you.

> Rupert Brooke

Why dust? A speck of dust to be exact, one speck. In it I was shown that God *is*. Amidst other knowledge (and unknowings) of Him, as many as the visible stars and the galaxies beyond our vision, for some reason God showed me His glory in dust. It was 1941.

This seeing moment was an unexpected gift that depended on nothing less (or else) than the '... covenant which is between you and every living creature ...' (Genesis 9.12,) which we read about in that story where God speaks to Noah – and all of us – about the rainbow:

> My bow I set in the cloud, sign of the covenant between myself and earth. When I cloud the sky over the earth, the bow shall be seen in the cloud.
> (9.13-14)

God's promise is to be fulfilled in His time, but the day he made the covenant with Noah was as he, his family and all living creatures came out of the ark on to dry land. Their imprisonment was over, their freedom beginning, and their fixed hope in a 'cloud of unknowing'. And dust was there in both rainbow and cloud. The seeing is a glimpse of eternity. Such moments demonstrate God in paradox: that which is unique is commonplace, that which happens once is of all time, that which is for one is for all. The meaning and heart of the paradox is always the mystery of love. Such moments are meant to be shared.

Julian of Norwich is a trusted guide in these matters, and I quote again from *Revelations of Divine Love*:

> We ought to rejoice in him then, both for what he shows and what he hides! And if we deliberately and humbly do this we shall experience great relief and earn his eternal gratitude . . . It is known that I have done miracles here in the past; many and marvellous, estimable and great. What I did then, I do still, and shall continue to do.
> (Ch.36)

Yes, this account is of such a momentary event.

PART III

Exult, O Dust and Ashes!

> Exult, O dust and ashes!
> The Lord shall be thy part:
> His only, His for ever
> Thou shalt be, and thou art!
>
> Bernard of Cluny, *Jerusalem the Golden*

I, wisdom . . . before the hills, came to birth: before he made the earth, the countryside, or the first grains of the world's dust . . .

Proverbs 8.12, 25-26

Polycarp (who might have known someone who knew Jesus!) wrote: 'Human nature cannot attain to the wisdom underlying all creation.'

Albert Einstein asked the question: Did God have the choice of beginning the universe? He also wrote, on 'Reconciliation':

> The most beautiful and most profound emotion we can experience is the sensation of the mystical. It is the sower of all true science. He to whom this emotion is a stranger, who can no longer wonder and stand wrapt in awe, is as good as dead. To know that what is impenetrable

to us really exists, manifesting itself in the highest wisdom and the most radiant beauty, which our dull faculties can comprehend only in their most primitive forms this knowledge, this feeling, is at the centre of true religiousness . . . My religion consists of a humble admiration of the illimitable superior Spirit, who reveals himself in the slight details we are able to perceive with our frail and feeble minds. That deeply emotional conviction of a superior reasoning power, which is revealed in the incomprehensible universe, forms my idea of God.

David Cecil wrote, in *Personal Anthology: Library Looking Glass*:

The most tremendous ending I know is that which closes Walton's life of John Donne: the spacious dead march off the penultimate paragraph and then following it, like a trumpet call, the brief triumphant last sentence:

He was earnest and unwearied in the search of knowledge; with which, his vigorous soul is now satisfied, and employed in a continual praise of that God, that first breathed it into his active body; that body, which was once a Temple of the Holy Ghost, and is now become a small quantity of Christian dust.
But I shall see it reanimated.

For birth hath in itself the germ of death
And death hath in itself the germ of birth.

Francis Thompson

We live together and we die together, wrote St Paul to the people at Corinth. But for five decades of the twentieth century death was hidden away and discussed as little as possible, forgotten as much as possible.

So much so has this been true that it could be called a phenomenal omission in my lifetime. However, we are coming out of that phase. It is the more remarkable in that we have seen so much through TV and satellite communications.

Was this silence about death necessary to obliterate the horror of the First World War? I believe that to be part of the explanation. The agony was too intense for memory. And paradoxically the impact has affected us all.

There was more agony to come.

My recollections of the late thirties are of how much and how variously conversations speculated on the European situation. How little one wanted to believe any of it. But another war came.

When it was over we did not speak of it. The word 'Hiroshima' had entered the language. I know what I was wearing, where I was sitting, when a friend came up and tried to explain what had happened. Nagasaki heaped on the pain. We no longer swapped our bomb stories or mentioned the deaths of friends or neighbours.

Soon appalling news of concentration camps began to filter through. We knew a little already, but the full shock and ghastliness came out slowly, and then so horrified us it was almost impossible to believe such hell had been let loose, and that so near a country in Europe could contain such experience: it was beyond any nightmare, anything anyone had ever imagined.

Slowly we learnt more and more: 'Pitchi Poi' – the song that the children sang as they were shoved into the gas chambers – was unbearable.

And then Stalin. Twenty million people wiped out?

Since then it has gone on. Wars – all around the globe. War in Vietnam, war in Nicaragua, West Africa, Ethiopia, the Falklands, Uganda, the Gulf, Yugoslavia and other places. On top of it all, atrocities in Romania and elsewhere, violence and shootings in Northern Ireland, the ever-present flash-point of the Middle East, and in South Africa injustices and the pain of apartheid. The number of millions involved in broken, tragic families. Droves of refugees, boatloads at sea.

And we watch all this pain happening.

Added to this the air crashes, disasters like Chernobyl and Bhopal that were unthought of, impossible, in my mother's childhood, or even mine. So much of the past 50, 40, 30, 20, 10 years contains shatteringly enormous changes.

It goes on. There is the ozone layer above us and the 'Harvest of Dust' created all around the globe, in a world that stockpiles butter, wheat and other foods and keeps lakes of wine. That is perhaps the worst pain of all. 'We live together: we die together.'

It doesn't end there. How changed the medical scene is since I had my tonsils out at the age of seven! So far, in fact, has the scene changed that it is almost unrecognisable.

A visit to just one ward – for instance, to see the premature babies. New children living who would once have died, while at the other end of life so many old people shuffling about. (Not so much of the shuffling, please!) And in between the young with Aids.

We talk about all this, we see it on the News, we are appalled, and yet we do not talk about death! We know it is happening all around us, but we dismiss it. We have to protect ourselves. Or is it possible to do something about it? We all ask ourselves this question, and maybe we have some answers. Yes, it is possible. By the way we live the life that is ours, uniquely, marvellously. All have opportunities and possibilities of using healing powers of kindness and understanding. We need to give and take encouragement, share problems. Mother Theresa, straight from the poverty and sickness of Calcutta, found Western loneliness a worse sickness.

Personal tragedies of bereavement are as they always have been, separate major events in our lives.

'The Lord is close to those who are broken-hearted; and the crushed in spirit he saves.' (Psalm 34.18) Blessed are those who know this is true.

In fact, mercifully, we have many groups of people helping each other now: Compassionate Friends, Cruse, bereavement counsellors and many more. Yes, the silence is being overcome.

But Friends of the Earth remind us that we have barely begun to care for our countryside, to save energy or even our whole planet. We waste water nearly every time we go to the loo, and turn lights on as though electricity were as available as daylight.

The dust of all the twentieth century death remains. Dust is its remains. Shall much rightly be swept away before the next millennium? Shall we sweep it under the carpet or recycle it in a more glorious future?

Dust – the symbol of death and the result of death itself. And yet we are still shy – self-conscious – about bringing it into our everyday talk. Why? Victorian children talked as normally about death as they did of their summer holidays.

I am old. My parents are dead. Friends have died. Neighbours have died. As I mentioned earlier, I was born in 1917, a year of appalling slaughter, the same week Charles Peguy was killed in France among hundreds of thousands. But some soldiers shouted three cheers for the Padre's daughter and made me a member of their mess aged one week. It was the only episode that my father mentioned about the trenches and that great war. The pain had set up barriers. The shadows fell all the time. The soldiers used to march down the road, past our garden hedge on their way to church from the barracks in Devizes. One day Tatie who was with me said, 'There are so few!' and turned away crying, leaving me there abandoned. It was the first time I saw a grown-up cry. I think I was three.

I experienced the Second World War, its devastation and the sickening sound of sirens – and the bombs. Counting out the V rockets. Swapping our tales. Making do on an egg a week and forgetting about bananas and oranges and much else. I know about grief and crushing sorrow. I do not come to write about dust and death as though they were forbidden subjects.

My aim is to make one point, state one belief: I believe that the moment of the incarnation shown in a speck of dust was to be a visual statement of the resurrection of the universe. Absolutely that!

My hope is that this concentration on the fact of dust has helped a little to remove the fear of death – or at least the difficulty of talking about it. We need to come to recognise that death points towards a new beginning; is something we can simply look forward to one day – dust transformed to glory.

So with faith and hope we end up knowing 'that the whole of life is grounded and rooted in love and without love we cannot live'.

'I have trouble with the word glory,' Mary said to me. Mary, a doctor, said that! With all her special wealth of experience of life, with her vivid imagination and, for a pastime, the most beautiful creative embroidery. But the word 'glory' was a problem for her.

And a few years later an elderly friend with an almost painfully developed imagination said: 'Just dust, not the word glory. I have difficulty with glory.'

Is this a common fear? That glory cannot be contained in a word? That God's glory so exceeds any experience in this life that we cannot dare to use it in language?

These two challenges forced me to rethink *Dust Glorified*. I had to come to a conclusion in order to expose my inner heart to an outward heart 'on the sleeve'. God, who is beyond language – the Aum – 'high above the heavens', asks us to acclaim him in everyday actions and situations. God who invented 30,000,000 insects as well as the galaxies (and earth is a speck in the galaxies) is present in the birth of each baby. That is where I came to the *end-point*. It was the birth of *that baby* to Mary in dark miserable circumstances that proclaimed glory and peace to mankind – the angels said so! And, believe it or not, so does dust.

It is not a matter of looking back.

Only he who has fought bravely and been victorious in the struggle against the spurious security and strength and attraction of the past can attain to the firm and blissful experiential certainty that the more we lose all foothold in the darkness and instability of the future, the more deeply we penetrate into God.

> Teilhard de Chardin, *Hymn to the Universe*

> Come down, O Lord divine,
> Seek thou this soul of mine,
> And visit with thine own ardour glowing;
> O, Comforter, draw near,
> Within my heart appear,
> And kindle it, thy holy flame bestowing.
>
> Oh let it freely burn,
> Till earthly passions turn
> To dust and ashes in its heat consuming
> And let thy glorious light
> Shine ever on my sight,
> And clothe me round, the while my path illuming.

> Bianca da Siena (15th Century)

Almighty and everliving God,
whose Son Jesus Christ healed the sick
and restored them to wholeness of life:
look with compassion on the anguish of the world,
and by your healing power
make whole both men and nations;
through our Lord and Saviour Jesus Christ,
who is alive and reigns with you and the Holy Spirit,
one God, now and for ever. Amen.

As this plait, this exercise in sharing, requires my own experiences, I would like to share two unexpected minutes that happened during two funerals.

Anne Coram's funeral was a very sad occasion. Her children were still young, her husband devastated. The church was full. The service had been worked out with immense care and many of her friends were involved in it. I was asked to read from Paul's Letter to the Romans, Chapter 8, at the end of the service. I had sat beside her in hospital for long hours just before she died, when her husband took over from me having put the children to bed.

During those long dark hours, I had the impression I was involved with all those deaths of our century which seem to bring us face to face with the *Why?* This sight of a young friend who had once said to me that, during her training as a doctor, she had spent a time in the St Christopher Hospice in London, where she had been deeply distressed by a young man who was brought in. She had said to herself: I hope I don't die like that. And that is what was happening.

The whole of my mind was immersed in this universally experienced *Why?* There was no answer except that I knew she had meant so much to me in life that she was also meaning a great deal in her death. I knew there was a meaning. It was something to do with the fact that when we talk about death we are usually talking about both death and the manner of death. Two quite different things. We are all afraid of the manner of our deaths. And we pray for courage when the time comes. But death – and what that means – is something else altogether.

It doesn't sound much to say we hang on to hope. But hope is as indestructible as the universe, even when it gets locked in a dark box, as Pandora knew. There has to be 'the hanging on'. The glory in dust without the agony of crucifixion would be an impoverished glory. And God does not require us to suffer more than we are able. Only Christ suffered all.

Only his crucifixion endured and encompassed all the whys.

I don't understand what I am saying, writing to you, but although I do not understand, I still can say: I know. And this conviction came home to me during Anne's funeral, and again later during the other one. Probably it has always been there in every funeral. I believe the funeral service itself is a great witness to the faith of Christians.

It was an ordeal to do the reading from Paul, which I could not refuse; but once I had started to read I was caught in his vision. I count it one of the great privileges of my life to have read this on her behalf. The reading ended:

> I am sure that neither death, nor life, nor
> angels, nor principalities, nor things present, nor
> things to come, nor powers, nor heights, nor
> depths, nor anything else in all creation, will be
> able to separate us from the love of God in Christ
> Jesus our Lord. (Romans 8.38-9)

It was some years later that something similar happened. Of course the circumstances were entirely different. Michael Hudson had been retired from being a doctor for some time, but had kept up an interest in everything around him. We had had wonderful talks, but sadly not during the few months before he died. His wife, Cicely, asked me to look through one of his notebooks with her and choose two readings for his funeral. This was to be in Bristol Cathedral. Again this was a service carefully planned, where the grandchildren took a lovely part, lighting candles. Again, it was an awesome occasion, but the congregation was full of very loving friends and a great number of people that he had helped in his lifetime along with the congregation of the Cathedral where he had worshipped. It is not hard to imagine how I felt, faced with a microphone. But again the readings completely took over and became all that was to be remembered. And if I quote them here it will not be hard to see why.

> Life limited by death? Nonsense! That is a great mistake. Death hardly counts, we already have eternal life and that should give us great tranquillity, as those who feel themselves to be eternal. Do not therefore be afraid of death. It is a flowering of life, the consummation of union with God.
>
> Abbé de Tourville, *Letters of Direction*

> As long as one can learn from the changes of life, one will never grow old in spirit. And the life beyond death will be the source of endless delight as one approaches its welcoming light at the end of a well-spent life on earth.
>
> Martin Israel

Christians call on special courage at funerals. Their grief is no less because they believe in eternity, but it is different.

A remarkably courageous widower just managed to read this at his wife's funeral:

The faith of Christ teaches more than courage in the face of death. Our attitude to death is transformed. As we come to a more intimate experience of the reality of God, we may enter into the overcoming power and strength of the great words of Christ: I am the resurrection and the life.

Death is swallowed up in victory. For those we love it is no longer a dark place of shadows but an entrance into the fuller light of God. Though we naturally grieve at the withdrawal of loved friends from our physical sight, we may still rejoice in their new freedom. The dead are not lost to us; they are still our friends in the service of the Eternal.

Of Joan Mary Fry to her friends, 1955

Perhaps 'Of course!' is what we shall find ourselves saying after we die and are in our new mode of existence.

Mrs B was telling me about her nephew and his wife:

They never go to church, dear, but I said to them, 'You want to have the service done properly,' and they said, 'Well, auntie, we had Dad taken to church so we'll do the same for Mum. You got us to have Dad taken,' they said, and do you know, dear, I think they were really glad they did take this decision. They said afterwards the best thing that I ever did for them was saying, 'Mind you have a service in church before the crem.' I don't know what I am myself, dear. I said to the Vicar, 'What do you think I am? I had an uncle who was a Catholic.' But the Vicar said, 'You are all right as you are, Mrs B, and it's a pity there aren't a lot more like you.' I was glad he said

that, it was nice of him. I've always said that
every minute was in His hands, and you have to
take the rough with the smooth. But He knows. I
think everybody would love him if they
understood. I know, I can't help it, dear, it goes
on in my head all the time. Would you like a bit
of shortbread to take back with you? I make
enough for my neighbour as well as myself. She
likes it and I like making it for her, as you don't
want much of it when you're on your own. It
crumbles easily – here, have a bit more, it keeps.
She won't mind; I'll tell her you called and we
had a nice chat; it's cheered me up no end – not
that I need cheering up, mind. I'm not that sort.
Of course, I can't get about like I used to, but you
don't feel as old as you are. I can still get to the
service in church, but if I can't, Vicar brings me
communion here. He's very kind.

'I expect it is a treat for him,' I said.

Opening one's eyes may take a life time, seeing is done
in a flash.

Anon.

'Mystical experience is notoriously difficult to
communicate in words,' wrote Richard Jefferies in his *The
Story of My Heart*. He also wrote:

> I have been obliged to write these things by an
> irresistible impulse which has worked in me since
> early youth. They have not been written for the
> sake of argument, still less for any thought of
> profit, rather indeed the reverse. They have been
> forced from me by earnestness of heart, and they
> express my most serious convictions.

These convictions have appeared often in the collecting of the anthology, *Dust Glorified*. It makes for an awareness of the wedding in Cana when Jesus showed that dirty water could also be good wine. And don't forget it was most certainly very dirty water. What was Jesus telling those guests on that occasion? And us today? The transformation was for joy.

So we return to our daily living:

> When all things common seem,
> When all is dust, and self the centre clod,
> When grandeur is a hopeless dream
> And anxious care more reasonable than God.
>
> Anon.

Dust can also represent depression, despair even – the great blackness when nothing but a turning of events can break the gloom ... Yes, we get despondent and gloomy.

We ask: does God love this world so much?

> Does God love the world
>   so
>   so much
> Or just so-so?
> You know?
> You know there is no such thing
> as so-so
> To God who loves the world
>   so
>   so much.

Is there help at hand? There is. Mother Julian understands how we feel coping with our everyday problems:

> In this blessed revelation of our Lord I begin to understand two very different things: the greatest

wisdom a man can attain in this life, and the greatest folly. The greatest wisdom is to fulfil the will and plan of his most exalted friend. This blessed friend is Jesus; it is his will and plan that we hang on to him, and hold tight always, in whatever circumstances; for whether we are filthy or clean is all the same to his love. He wants us never to run away from him, whether things are going well or ill. But because our self is so changeable we often fall into sin. And then we are influenced by our enemy and our blind folly.

'See,' they say, 'you are a wretched creature, a sinner, and a liar to boot. You do not keep God's commandments. You are always promising our Lord to do better, and then you immediately go and fall again into the same sin – and particularly into sloth, and time wasting.' It looks to me as though sin begins here, especially in the case of those who have given themselves to serve our Lord contemplatively, gazing at his blessed goodness. And this makes us dread appearing before our courteous Lord. Thus would our enemy set us back with this false dread of our wretchedness, and the pain he threatens us with. He means to make us so despondent and weary that we forget all about the lovely blessed sight of our everlasting friend. (Ch.76)

To dwell on dust would be absurd, as if one thought about it as one breathes. In fact one never thinks about breathing it. Only in the sunbeam are we aware of its perpetual motion.

Its own silence has something to tell us – silence is so much part of nature's lessons. Nature's glimpses are available to everyone, even, hopefully, for those living in the concrete jungles.

So for the 'dull' days, the distressed days, the empty

days, surely there are simple old-time cures to turn to and find reliable?

1. The Bible close at hand, both with commentaries from the theologians, various translations, and our inner eye, trusting the latter.

    a) Remembering that the people of Corinth were just a cross-section crowd you might find at any busy port.

    b) I was staggered to open the Bible at Esdras recently, since the Gulf war began, and read the second book. It might have won the Booker Prize and cost £19. It read like a thriller.

    c) Or if you want to find God as a crocodile, try Job (40.15–41.34, NEB). Read Job from time to time in any case. God brought him through his tribulations.

Oh! the Bible. Old and New Testaments. Translated in all the languages of the world, and constantly under scrutiny to reveal more and more truths of the past, present and future.

2. Making friends with spiritual writers. Having a particular one to turn to.

But here I feel compelled to quote from Ronnie Knox's introduction to Thomas à Kempis's book, *The Imitation of Christ*:

> If a man tells you he is fond of the *Imitation*, view him with sudden suspicion; he is either a dabbler or a saint. No manual is more pitiless in its exposition of the Christian ideal, less careful to administer consolation by the way.

And he ends the preface:

The whole work was meant to be, surely, what it is – a sustained irritant which will preserve us if it is read faithfully, from sinking back into relaxation; from self-conceit, self-pity, self-love. It offers consolation here and there, but always at the price of fresh exertion, of keeping your head pointing upstream. Heaven help us if we find easy reading in the *Imitation of Christ*.

It seems a salutary warning which may apply to other books in spite of most writers trying to make God's love more easily available.

3. There is a place for recalling happy memories from the past, especially those moments which nature has given us. A sunset, a dawn chorus, the sound of kittiwakes in a far-off place, or even seagulls raking over a refuse dump.

Here is a memory I shall never forget. A friend and I parked the car and set out to walk across the Clifton Downs about three o'clock on a sunny November day. It was extraordinarily beautiful, the sun coming down to embrace the earth. We then saw a sight I had never seen before, or quite the same since.

The grass had grown to about six inches high, and it shimmered with a look of water, as the sea can appear at a low tide on a huge wide beach, very calm and shallow.

It so shimmered one hesitated to put a foot down, it seemed sacrilege to walk on such beauty. The sinking sun was shining on a network of billions of lightly dew-covered spiders' web threads.

When I got out of the car on reaching home again, I noticed that my shoes were covered in a horrid mess of cobwebs. That this was the same as the exquisitely beautiful threads on the Downs was quite simply incredible.

For every cobweb, for every speck of dust, there is a

truth waiting to be revealed. The whole universe is perpetually poised in waiting for us to realise Something – *God knows how.*

'God knows how' – say it reverently and with awe, not angrily, blasphemously, in exasperation or disbelief.

Take the words of Jesus Christ to heart: Consider the lilies of the field.

4. Collecting favourite quotations, cuttings that interest, pictures that inspire, poems that convey Otherness. I have shared with you from my hoard.

5. Or pursuing whatever brings you happiness. Perhaps it is music, painting, sewing, cooking, gardening, walking, having friends for a cup of tea. Anything creative tends to resurrection!

And if you are young, a thousand visions, journeys, adventures may be yours, perhaps without doing anything different from whatever you have to do today.

6. May you count it a blessing to be bored, to have dull days, empty days, and find the happiness of learning to fill them – without switching on the TV. This suggestion is not for children: we should all help them not to suffer the ills of boredom.

7. How about doing a spot of dusting?

8. And pray. Give thanks for everyone who has helped us to understand the love of God. Pray for those we are drawn to pray for, should pray for . . . And remember to pray for sewage workers, the 'dustbin' men, everyone who keeps the world a cleaner, lovelier place. And for ourselves going round with the duster again.

Dusting

The dust comes secretly day after day
Lies on my ledges and dulls my shining things
But, O this dust that I shall drive away
Is flowers and kings
Is Solomon's Temple, poets, Nineveh.

Alice Meynell

Another memory reminds me of something very important to say. Perhaps it should have been said at the start.

This description – this attempt at sharing – my experience of *Dust Glorified* is not really important for you – though I thought when I decided to write about it that it might be. Now I see that it is only in one aspect important, that is, to confirm you in your own realisation of God's loving, constant presence with you and with us all. And in all creation. 'Let all the world in every corner sing!'

You will have had and will have your own moments. There is no life without a sudden realisation of Otherness in it – though often forgotten. When you were a child you saw a flower, a feather or a flea for the first time. You met a stranger who looked at you with a loving eye, or even with a warm hand on yours. Perhaps television brought you some moment of unutterable wonder. A moment of wonder and insight. It was unexpected. It came 'out of the blue'. Some children have too little experience of love, but for them it should be as prevalent as dust.

I once had the privilege of watching a four-year-old child see her first daffodil. It was on a window-sill in a tenement building.

(Such buildings should not have existed in the 1950s. They were built inhumanly by the Boards of Directors who ran the railway companies. The best that could be said of them is that they meant well. Or did they? Were families, human beings, ever intended to live like that? One thing is sure: none of those directors would have done so! The tenements were built in the 1880s, pronounced unfit by the 1920s and condemned, but left in use until 1960. Yes, it makes you angry. Forty years of children should never have grown up there. I heard many people say: 'I had no idea such places existed.' But they did, and Patsy and her family were among those that lived in Barnham Street Buildings, London.)

On the day of Patsy's happiness, I was sitting inside with these flower pots perched precariously on the outside. The window was so grey with dirt and grime that the child could not see me inside. (It was no use cleaning windows when the trains went by every minute.) It was such a grey, filthy place that I could barely see the child herself. Patsy was on her way home from playing on the bombed site with her sister who hadn't gone to school – she was minding Patsy because Mum had taken the baby to hospital. They enjoyed playing on the bombed site, building jumping-off places, and throwing stones. She was on her way home, up the stone staircase to the two rooms where she lived with her three sisters and beautiful Italian mother and hard-working father. Perhaps I should make the point that five 'flats' shared one tap and sink under the stairs, a much broken and chipped sink at that. And they shared two lavatories. Just imagine! These were often out of use. There were five landings altogether and the same dust chute for all. Patsy took it all for granted, she had never known anything else. Even so, all the children hated the stench. I knew Patsy and her family well, and all the other children and the many old people – in fact, we all knew each other more or less. But I was lucky. I didn't live there. I shared a tiny terraced house round the corner with three friends. It's true it was surrounded on three sides by bombed sites and an old-fashioned printing house on the fourth. But we had our own outside loo, and a bath in the kitchen. The children thought we lived in luxury. 'Cor, wish we 'ad 'n 'ouse like you'm got,' they said.

Back in the buildings I sat in the little two-roomed flat where one room was called 'eroffice'. There was a desk and a 'pianner', a telephone and paraphernalia for the children to play with, lots of it, and this mildewy cupboard where the children had planted and watered some lanky daffodils. It was a miracle that they had survived. The first day they flowered, I put them on the window ledge outside. Old Mr Curtis had died or he would have been using it to prop himself up on, with his one leg, and get some gossip. Outside was a concrete yard with enormous containers that the dust chutes emptied into and ended up overspilling by the end of each week. We welcomed the dustbin men, even when they hurried off without sweeping up. But it was George and his son Georgie who got them working and unjammed the chutes and mended the window sashes and broken windows, taps, steps and countless other things. 'Seen George?'

'Cor, you'm daft,' said George, 'leaving them flowers by the winder. They'll be nicked.'

'Not by the children,' I said. 'I'm taking a chance on the others.'

'Good luck!' he said, which in that place always meant 'Yer poor thing'!

Patsy was on her way home from the bombed site. The schoolchildren were yet to come. As she rounded the corner and saw the five daffodils, she stopped. She stood on tiptoe and looked down the first trumpet. 'I love you,' she said. And then to each one, 'I love you. I love you. I love you. I love you.' Then a voice from far above called her: 'Come on up, Pats.'

The next morning the daffodils were still there. But not the next. 'Told yer so,' said George. But I didn't mind. Patsy had had her glimpse of eternity.

I didn't mean to make such a long account of it. But the fact is I dreamed of the buildings last night. I was happy there. But I'm glad it was a dream and that I actually saw them being pulled down. Now that was the filthiest dust you ever saw. I am not romantic about dust. All the more do I wonder at this glorification. And know that God is in every experience of the world.

For those who fear the impossibility of such things, there is always one way through their tunnel. It is to believe that it is a tunnel. That there is a light at the end. That it is worth waiting, that it is wise to be open to all new ideas, all new impressions. Perhaps God is providing us with as many millions of miracles as shining dewdrops, each with its own rainbow, and as many human hearts thirsting for such dew.

If the sheer immensity of his love overwhelms us, stretches our belief into unbelief, it will return in moments of time that are unique to each one of us. God is love. Every moment of 'love is his meaning'.

That's how Julian ended her book. For me these four words have become something more than a beautiful bow to tie on the end of a plait.

Appendix

The following is taken from a letter from Dr Nigel Metcalfe, who took the photograph entitled 'Stars':

The picture was taken by putting a very sensitive electronic camera on the end of the 100-inch Isaac Newton telescope (which lives in the Canary Islands) and opening the shutter for 24 hours (not all at once of course!) – in practice only a few hours are exposed each night and it all has to be added together at the end.

What it shows are several thousand faint galaxies, many virtually at the edge of the visible universe – and note that a galaxy is a collection of about 100 thousand million stars like our sun, but these galaxies are so distant that all we see is one little white speck for each galaxy. To give some idea of scale, if you look at the full moon, then the long side of the photographic covers about 1/5 of the moon's apparent diameter – so it is a really tiny patch of sky! And the faintest galaxies you can see on the photograph are about 200 million times fainter than the faintest star you can see with the naked eye (and that's faint! – in fact these are the faintest objects ever photographed). Of course, all of them were formed from gas and dust, and many (or their component stars) are destined to turn to dust when they die.

To sum up, a suitable caption would be: The ultimate origin of dust – a look-back over 10 billion years to when the universe was young. The photograph, man's deepest yet look into space, shows the sky dappled with thousands of faint galaxies at the edge of the observable universe.

Oh, and by the way, the purpose of all this is to count the number of galaxies and compare with that what you would expect if our Milky Way were a typical galaxy – and what you would find is that galaxies must have been much brighter and/or more numerous in the past. But that's another story . . .